The Creativity Playbook
For Lawyers

Strategies for the Business of Legal Practice

First Edition

Adam Tsao | Legal Beta

Legal Beta LLC
Falls Church, Virginia 22040
Copyright © 2021 by Adam Tsao

First Legal Beta LLC paperback edition March 2021.

Published under At Philosophy (registered trademark).

For information about special discounts for bulk purchases, please contact Legal Beta at 202-810-9928 or at www.legalbeta.xyz.

For more information about speaking engagements, workshops, or to book an event, contact Legal Beta at 202-810-9928 or at www.atphilosophy.com.

Cover and interior design by Legal Beta LLC.

Manufactured in the United States.

Library of Congress Control Number: 2021902879

ISBN 978-0-578-85842-5

Adam Tsao

ADAM TSAO is the founder of Legal Beta, a company dedicated to driving innovation in the legal industry through creativity workshops, coaching, and consulting.

Adam practiced corporate law in Washington, D.C. at Covington & Burling LLP and, prior to that, at Skadden, Arps, Slate, Meagher & Flom LLP. Across both firms, he advised on domestic and international transactions. As part of his pro bono practice, he counseled nonprofits and social-enterprise startups on corporate structuring and mergers and acquisitions. Prior to law, Adam was a commercial real estate broker with Jones Lang LaSalle Inc. where he managed the development of a geo-spatial analytics platform in the Mid-Atlantic region.

He graduated law school from the University of Pennsylvania School of Law, where he received the Wharton Certificate in Management, served on the executive board of the Journal of Business Law, and led both the Financial Literacy Project and the Urban Ventures Project. He also conducted research at the Wharton School on the intersectionality of innovation and law. Adam graduated college from Washington University in St. Louis, with a major in philosophy and a minor in psychology.

Adam resides in the Washington, D.C. metropolitan area and serves as president of the Asian Pacific American Bar Association Educational Fund, an at-large board member of the Penn Club of D.C., and a D.C. advisory board member of the Network for Teaching Entrepreneurship.

Learn more about his work at www.legalbeta.xyz.

The Creativity Playbook
For Lawyers

Strategies for the Business of Legal Practice

First Edition

Adam Tsao | Legal Beta

For the next generation.

Contents

PART I: BUILDING THE FOUNDATION

§1
Introduction

For the practice of law.

The Creativity Playbook for Lawyers is designed to serve as a resource for attorneys to think about their practice from the business perspective and to apply creative problem-solving principles to their workflow. As a baseline, it's important to remember that law firms and legal teams are businesses and business units. This point can sometimes elude us because the industry tends to focus myopically on the subject matter without the appropriate counterbalance of the actual *practice* of such subject matter. For instance, we are trained in contract drafting and brief writing at the outset of our legal careers, but we aren't trained to drive procedural efficiencies, manage teams, or build a client base. Rather than brushing this problem (and others like it) off as a "bschool" problem, it can be exceedingly beneficial to address the business of practice head on. Through the power of creative problem solving, this playbook seeks to provide you with the fundamental tools to improve the business of your practice, whether you are a junior or senior attorney.

The structure of this playbook is as follows. In this Part I, I provide a general foundation for creative problem solving in legal practice, which will help establish the necessary guideposts, address any pre-conceived notions about what it means to be creative (especially as an attorney), and level set expectations. In Part II, I provide a breakdown of eleven creative problem-solving strategies that can be applied to legal practice. Each strategy has its own dedicated section, which is divided into an overview section to explain how the approach works generally and an application section to provide you with a sample, step-by-step guide of how you can implement the approach in practice. These sections are designed for quick referencing so that you can quickly flip to the appropriate strategy when needed, and they can be read independently of one another. Afterwards, in Part III, I share a few parting perspectives on creative problem solving for legal practice. And lastly, in the Appendix, I include creativity exercises to help you practice creative thinking. Creativity is a group effort, so pull together your friends and walk through the exercises together. Have some fun, share crazy and wild ideas, and enjoy the process.

As you begin to develop your creative skillset, allow yourself the opportunity to venture into unfamiliar waters. Once you do, you can learn to embrace your creativity to become a better team player, a better leader, and a better attorney.

§2
A Creative Foundation

Where it all begins.

§2.1: Why Creativity Matters in the Law

There is a French term known as *déformation professionnelle*, which refers to how people tend to view the world from the vantage point of their profession, training, or area of expertise.[1] It is a cognitive bias that prevents people from taking a broader view of the present scenario. This affects attorneys in one of two ways. First, we may unknowingly and unintentionally overemphasize the legal significance of certain points without adequately translating our analysis into business terms for our clients. If your client asks "what does that mean for the business" or asks you to translate what you just said into "layman's terms," you've gone too far on the legalize. Second, when we focus too much on the legal aspects of our practice, we can lose sight of what it means to be part of a business. When you walk into your doctor's office or into a hospital, what do you normally complain about? The logistics. The process of scheduling an appointment was difficult, the wait time was too long, ordering a prescription was inconvenient, or the transition between attending physicians wasn't seamless. The pressure points typically aren't with the physicians themselves – it's with the business of how their practice or the hospital is run. Why? Because physicians aren't trained to be operators – they are trained to be medical advisors.

The same is true in law. Clients typically complain about how our legal teams operate in delivering the client experience versus the actual quality of the legal product and analysis. Why? Because effective lawyering moves beyond researching the black letter law; effective lawyering requires strategic advocacy – and this is where creative problem solving can make a substantial impact for your clients, your legal team, and yourself. "Best practices" in the legal industry are too often the equivalent of "prior practices." This is terrible. We need to flip this presumption arrow from backward facing to forward facing. Creative problem solving does just this. It refocuses the legal mind towards the business of legal practice. It counteracts the perspective atrophy that is all too prevalent in the profession. Take a moment to think about the below list of questions.

- How can your legal team enhance existing practices to promote efficiency within your team?
- How can you maximize efficiency under alternative fee arrangements (e.g., fixed-fee arrangements)?
- How can your legal team differentiate itself from competitors and drive the bottom line?
- How is your legal team promoting diversity and inclusion?
- How is your legal team supporting attorney well-being?
- How can your legal team improve attorney retention, better train your attorneys, and build a robust pipeline of talent?
- What can your legal team do differently to improve client interactions?
- How are your clients *experiencing* their interactions with your team and what can be improved?
- What are you doing to crowdsource innovation from your legal team?

Applying a creative mindset towards your legal practice can help answer questions like these with actionable solutions. Notice, also, that these questions aren't phrased to elicit "yes" or "no" responses. How we phrase our questions and define our problems are as important as the solutions themselves. Solving an incorrect problem moves you backwards; however, revealing the correct problem, even without an immediate solution, moves you forward. Businesses, such as law firms, that are able to define the correct problems or opportunities can thus better position themselves to develop a value-creating action plan. Often, the right problem or opportunity is also the more complex one. This is why the businesses that opt to take the harder path tend to build the strongest foundations. No one thought online shopping would be a thing. No one thought getting into strangers' vehicles would catch on. And no one thought that renting out their homes like hotels would work. The harder path won out.

And if you haven't considered the above questions before, that's okay. We are all on the journey of continuous learning and improvement. It is, however, important for you to take a moment to ask yourself why you haven't thought about these questions before. One key reason may be because you weren't trained to think about the *practice of law*. You were only trained to think about *the law itself*. Creative thinking expands your mind beyond your traditional training and education so that you can create more value all around.

This is now more important than ever because the legal industry is on the precipice of rapid change. Technology is set to disrupt how the law is practiced with the development of more advanced artificial intelligence programs, project management systems, and advanced research databases. Client values are evolving as clients demand their advisors to share the same level of commitment to causes like diversity and inclusion and innovation as they are. Business standards are changing as the world is becoming faster and more connected. And attorney preferences are changing. Partnership is no longer a top priority for many young attorneys as work-life balance becomes more highly valued. Fundamentally, the business of law is rapidly changing and the legal teams that fail to evolve will disappear. Legal teams can no longer rely on the inertia of their past successes to carry them forward. You can either double down on the gas-powered automobile or invest in the next generation of electric vehicles. The change is inevitable as the legal industry is one of the last verticals to be truly disrupted, in part due to its strategically conservative, reactive approach to market changes. But as market pressures for disruption and innovation increase, legal teams will either be crushed by the weight due to an inability to adapt or they will be forged into something stronger because of their ability to evolve. Legal teams must be creative and view these changes as an opportunity to capture greater value for their clients and their team. Phrased in the positive, legal teams that are able to develop more creative attorneys will create a foundation of innovation that will position them at the forefront of the next era in law.

Just think. As the legal market stands, innovation and change are driven by business clients. The huge push for diversity and inclusion came from clients incentivizing more diverse teams through bonus structures (or disincentivizing a lack of diversity through penalties). What if your legal team didn't wait for your clients to demand change? What if your legal team became the industry standard for innovation? What if your legal team took the initiative to address the hard problems? You would win the hearts of clients and be the beacon of what a legal team could be.

To address the elephant in the room: are lawyers even creative? After all, creativity and the law seem to be antithetical concepts reflective of the right brain versus left brain distinction. But I have a secret for you: we all have one brain that consists of two halves. Those halves? The so-called "right brain" and the so-called "left brain." So yes, you have access to both! You may be more left-brain analytical, but this doesn't mean that you can't apply right-brain creativity to your practice. All lawyers have the potential to be extremely creative. These creative qualities just express themselves differently than in traditionally defined "creative" professions like music. Why? Because creativity in the law is a means to an analytical end: an agreement or a brief. This relationship is flipped for musicians because they use analytical techniques (e.g., mathematically based music theory) to produce creative work products: music. In practice, lawyers do engage in some level of creative problem solving. All parties are playing by the same set of rules: the law. To advocate more effectively on behalf of a client, lawyers, then, must creatively problem solve with asymmetric factual information. This playbook serves to tap into that creative potential and refocus it into full view.

Law firms are businesses and legal teams are business units. In this service-based industry, having the best legal knowledge doesn't translate into having the best business. As it stands, more attorneys need to think about their practice from the business perspective. The practice of law is focused on client service, and client service can always be improved. The legal industry, from the business perspective, is slow to change. But those that can adapt a creative approach to their practice can position themselves to improve their bottom line and strengthen their businesses. A law firm or legal team that can embrace and apply creativity to their practice can build a great economic "moat" for itself to insulate and protect its business.[2]

In a study conducted by McKinsey & Company, businesses that are more creative outperform their peers on key financial metrics. Specifically, 67% of creative businesses had above-average organic revenue growth, 70% had above-average total return to shareholders, and 74% had above-average net enterprise value. Business that are less creative show the opposite results – they were significantly less likely to show above-average financial results.[3] Further, many surveys have shown that businesses consistently rank creativity as one of the most valued skills for employees to possess.[4] With both of these findings as context, it is interesting, but not surprising, that legal leaders have not sought to promote creativity within their ranks. It's not only time to drive creativity in law, it's also inevitable. The decision, then, is not whether creativity will benefit you and your team. The decision is whether to adapt a creative mindset before your competitors. The decision is to lead or be left behind.

§2.2: Open-Mindedness

Open-mindedness is fundamental to creativity. Without being open to trying new things or learning new things, we can't push the needle forward. In practice, being open-minded will allow us to dive into different disciplines, question the status quo, address the sticky questions, and drive new initiatives. This last point is particularly important because attorneys tend to dislike novelty. Why is this the case? Likely because legal precedence holds a special place in our legal system. Legal precedence, though, is drastically different than the precedence of practice. One deals with the inherent value of equal justice under the law; the other deals with how legal advising is conducted. The two should not be conflated, but, in practice, they predominantly are. This operational conservatism has meant that the legal industry has remained largely unchanged over the years, which creates a material limitation to providing greater value for clients and attorney teams.

Just because signing and closing checklists have been done the same way for the past decade doesn't mean that process can't be improved upon. Just because we send emails with dozens of marked-up attachments to clients (and internally) doesn't mean that's the best method of managing client (and internal) interactions. Chances are that you've heard your colleagues express their frustration over how archaic certain procedures are. Or, maybe you are the one that voices your opinions. But, then, why don't we see more changes or improvements? Because attorneys aren't trained in the art of business. They aren't trained to implement organizational change. They are trained in the art of legal research, analysis, and advocacy. Junior attorneys aren't encouraged to find better ways of doing things; they are encouraged to find precedent and conform to that precedent. And, traditionally, when a junior attorney becomes senior enough to have a voice, he or she will be too busy figuring out what business development actually means and running deals or cases to devote enough time to look for true best practices. Important business items like creative problem solving and value creation gets lost in all the noise.

Additionally, how many times have you heard someone say: well what did XYZ firm do? No one wants to be the "first" to do anything in the law and firms look to each other before making any material decisions – take attorney compensation at the largest firms as an example. Dozens of the largest firms move to the same compensation structure within weeks – even days – of one another. It's crazy. For clarity, conducting your market diligence is a vital part to good decision making. But relying on market diligence as a means to conformity is not. See what your peers are doing and follow that task up with a question: how can we lead the pack?

To be successful in the next era of legal practice, attorneys and legal teams will need to break free from their reactionary habits. They will need to open their minds and become innovators, and they will need to ban the phrase "well what did XYZ firm do?" from business conversations. Don't be afraid to try something new, stand out, and take ownership of your future. As Beau Lotto, a neuroscientist and founder of Lab of Misfits, states: "Creativity comes from not knowing. We do almost everything to avoid uncertainty, but the irony is that that is the only place we can go to see differently."[5] And, as the late Tony Hsieh remarks: "…I don't know whether predictability is actually an advantage. I think that's how organizations get stuck, because they want that predictability of structure. But if it's the wrong structure, what's the benefit of being predictably wrong?"[6]

An important corollary to open-mindedness and venturing into creative territory is an ability to accept failure. Creative problem solving requires a certain openness to try and experiment with new methodologies, but it also requires a certain level of risk tolerance. It's important for legal teams to understand that experimenting with something new doesn't mean that that experiment is set in stone – it doesn't automatically become precedent...it just helps inform future decisions. And you will make mistakes, but mistakes are a pathway towards success – and your clients are likely positioned to appreciate your efforts regardless of the outcome because innovation and experimentation are so well regarded on the business front.

Relatedly, embarking on any new process may leave you feeling a sense of uncertainty or doubt. This is actually a good sign because this means that you are venturing into new territory. You are learning and you are growing. Remember that gut feeling on your first day of law school...nervous about whether you would be called on or not? Remember that same feeling during your first day as a real attorney? Uncertainty and doubt are the precursor to improvement. As Tony Fadell, the designer known as the "father of the iPod" and the co-founder of Nest, notes: "If you aren't having doubt, you aren't pushing the boundaries far enough."[7]

As you begin to build your creative foundation, keep in mind that this is not meant to displace or replace your legal training – it's meant to accentuate it. Just as developing business savvy can heighten your legal practice, so, too, can developing a creative toolkit. Establishing a creative foundation requires us to be open to trying new things, to be open to listening to and collaborating with more people, to be open to taking risk, and to be open to experimenting with novelty.

Once your creative foundation begins to solidify, it will become a professional asset with compound interest. By tapping into your team's and your creative potential, you can crowdsource innovation to address matters of client management, firm citizenship, attorney well-being, business positioning, and effective lawyering.

§2.3: Structuring Creativity and Innovation

Structuring creativity and innovation within your team and organization is critically important for ensuring continued ideation and action. Without it, you will only be able to develop spurts of one-off ideas and solutions. The goal is to establish a creativity flywheel that builds momentum as your team strengthens its creativity muscle.

The first step, which is often the hardest, is to introduce the concept of creative thinking to your team and to train them to apply it. In legal practice, attorneys are on the front lines. They are advising on the ground and they are driving the bottom line; they are creating the market trends through their deals and their cases; and they have their hands on their clients' pulses. If you can train your attorneys to be more creative, to look for business opportunities, and to think beyond their immediate practice, your legal team can strengthen its market positioning.

In tandem with training your attorneys, providing creativity training to the staff is also critically important. The staff provides the backbone to any team or organization by allowing attorneys to focus on maximizing their billable time on the front lines. Moreover, staff members tend to have longer tenures at firms and organizations than the attorneys themselves, which gives them a unique perspective on how the team has progressed over time. As such, the staff and the attorneys must be in sync for new ideas and innovative measures to take effect. For instance, staff members may be aware of certain workflow inefficiencies within the team or organization but they may not have the right channel to voice their ideas (e.g., the staff may raise an idea with the attorneys who in turn punt the idea to another discussion in the future…in perpetuity…does this ring any bells?). Or it may be that the staff members will need to collaborate with the attorneys to drive a new initiative like improving procedures for timekeeping and managing expenses. Creative problem solving isn't reserved for a select few, it's a powerful tool that requires everyone to be involved.

After training your attorneys and staff, the second step is to put in place the appropriate structures and support networks within your organization to effect new ideas. Without these structures in place, there will only be spurts of one-off ideas. You can hold regular workshops and trainings to instill a creative mindset to your team, but without business channels in place for your team to practice and voice their creativity, forward progress will be limited. To consistently produce creative, value-generating ideas, teams need processes and platforms that encourage creativity and innovation. If you are in a position to establish channels of ideation by, for example, creating monthly creativity meetings or a creativity committee to liaise across the team or organization, your task is to implement these channels. If you aren't in a position where you can make these implementations, your task is to generate enough buy-in from decision makers to structure such creative thinking. Start small, show that the process works, and build from that foundation. For instance, schedule a coffee break with a senior team member and share with her some of your ideas. Over time, suggest inviting different members from your team to share their ideas with her as well. This organic process can jumpstart a thoughtful and impactful discussion to improve and evolve your practice.

Just as promoting personal fitness is improved by having ready access to workout equipment and recreational areas, promoting creativity is improved by having the appropriate organizational mechanisms in place to translate the problem-solving potential of your team into long-term benefits. This is exactly why the most innovative businesses in the world are able to continually innovate – they are built for it, literally.

Of course, certain industries like tech are naturally designed for creativity. Computer engineers and designers are constantly developing new products with new features. They find better ways for us to interact with information and they make life easier. The culture of tech firms is innovation and they have the appropriate platforms in place to let their talent flourish. Other industries, on the other hand, like the law are not built for innovation prima facie. Legal practice is traditionally rigid with practitioners that are accustomed to a certain way of conducting business. Our challenge, then, is actually an opportunity: to introduce and drive creativity and innovation in the legal field.

§2.4: Overview of Creative Problem-Solving Strategies

Creative problem solving as a practice is not new. It's been around for some time. The design and technology industries were the first to adapt this concept into their practices, and other industries like consumer goods, retail, fashion, medicine, and finance have followed suit. The legal industry, however, remains behind the curve. Creativity and innovation in the legal industry means something very different than in other industries. After all, attorneys aren't designing spaceships to Mars or life-saving technologies. Legal creativity is about finding ways to better improve the act of providing legal counsel – both for the client and the attorney.

In Part II, I discuss eleven creative problem-solving strategies that can be applied to legal practice. Each strategy will have its own section that will be broken up into two parts: (i) an overview subsection that characterizes the strategy, and (ii) an application subsection that provides sample steps that can help you think through applying the strategy to your fact-specific situation. As this playbook is meant to serve as a reference for your practice, each section can be read independently of one another.

As an overview, these eleven strategies are introduced below.

1. **Question the status quo.** One of the best places to start is by questioning the status quo. In debate and argumentation, this strategy is akin to questioning the premise. Just because something is done a certain way, it's always important for us to ask why something is the way it is and whether that something can be improved upon. This strategy is commonly discussed but rarely practiced in reality.
2. **Identify pressure points.** Where are your pressure points? Perhaps your organizational skills are lagging behind your analytical skills. Or perhaps networking and business development aren't your cup of tea. Relatedly, where are your team's pressure points? Do you need additional administrative support? Is your

team billing efficiently? By identifying your pressure points, you can better devote resources towards self-improvement or strengthening your team.

3. **Generate more ideas.** Generating new and creative ideas is a numbers game. The more ideas you generate, the greater your probability of coming up with something valuable. It's sort of like mining for gold. The greater your search area, the greater your probability of success. Whether you choose to write your ideas down in a notebook, notepad, whiteboard, or app, taking the time to generate more ideas can significantly increase your chances of developing the best strategy for you and your team. At best, this strategy can lead to capturing value in a way no one has considered before. At worst, you've created optionality. Not a bad outcome either way.

4. **Develop diverse teams.** By pulling together a team of people with diverse backgrounds (e.g., professional, cultural, racial, gender, age, disability, hierarchal), you can develop strategies that a homogeneous group could never come up with. Additionally, your ideas will be more robust and creative because you'll be discussing topics from multiple, differing vantage points. For example, when you are building a new home, you may wish to use the builder's established team of architects, engineers, electricians, and plumbers. Anything less, and you might find yourself with faulty electrical lines and toilets that don't flush properly. At the same time, if you wanted a more unique home, you could hire an architect and an interior designer with experiences in international design to create a truly one-of-a-kind home. Business initiatives are the same way. Having the requisite set of skills is a must and bringing in different backgrounds will help you create more exciting services, products, and initiatives. For practice, this includes hiring staff to help lead and coordinate internal initiatives rather than leaving certain responsibilities to the attorneys, who are already time limited (e.g., bringing on chief diversity officers and chief innovation officers).

5. **Embrace interdisciplinary thinking.** Similar to developing diverse teams, embracing interdisciplinary thinking can lead to immensely more powerful ideas than static thinking. By engaging in interdisciplinary fields, you can increase your chances of having that "Dr. House" moment when he miraculously connects two seemingly disjointed ideas to save his patient's life. Further, take a moment to think about leaders in your field, whether the CEO, founder, or managing partner of your company or one of the rock stars in your field – they, more often than not, brought something unique to the table that their peers weren't able to do. Embrace

other disciplines and dive into your quarks.

6. **Learn from all parts of your business.** Smaller businesses tend to be better at innovating because they are nimbler than larger ones. They are also better at innovating because their teams interact more frequently. At a large, Fortune 500 company, you can walk into the office and never have a conversation with someone outside of your team. At a small company, on the other hand, you can have a conversation with Joe in marketing and Jane in accounting all in the same afternoon because you sit within shouting distance of one another. This allows you to get broader perspectives of what is going on at the company because different teams have different vantage points. By applying this logic to larger organizations, listening to employees from across the company (both horizontally and vertically) can help you gather better ideas than if you only kept ideation to management. This also includes soliciting feedback from clients and employees. Positive feedback is great. It provides us with an ego boost. But negative feedback is where the money is, literally, because resolving the source(s) of this negative feedback can lead to immediate financial benefits. Clients may uncover the hidden truth behind a particular service or product that you thought was great but wasn't in reality. They can also highlight weaknesses in your offerings that you never noticed. At the same time, getting feedback from employees is equally important. They are your family. Your employees are spending the majority of their days working for you and with you. If they have concerns or ideas, it's important to make a good-faith effort in giving your employees a voice. Your employees are your greatest asset. Don't try to create ideas in a vacuum. Open yourself up to the feedback of others.

7. **Implement an "ideas-first" practice vs. "seniority-first" practice.** When seniority is valued above the idea, teams are disincentivized from generating new ideas or questioning the status quo. The organization, as a result, will remain stagnant. On the other hand, when ideas are valued over seniority, teams are incentivized to develop more thoughtful and impactful ideas. By promoting the value of ideas, at all levels, you can simultaneously crowdsource ideas from your team, encourage ideation, and increase the morale of your organization. There will be times when executive decision-making is required, but brainstorming is an inclusive process – not an exclusive one. This strategy requires some emotional intelligence as well because egos need to be kept in check. We have to be comfortable with someone else coming up with the defining idea or solution. We also have to be comfortable with being called out by our juniors. It's not about fighting for

credit; it's about fighting for the best idea for the team and organization.

8. **Implement design thinking.** The brilliant minds at IDEO have made design thinking mainstream. I recommend *Creative Confidence* by David M. Kelley (the founder of IDEO) and his brother Tom Kelley. This process focuses on humancentric design. It's a creative problem-solving method that consists of six different phases: (i) frame a question, (ii) gather inspiration, (iii) generate ideas, (iv) make ideas tangible, (v) test to learn, and (vi) share the story.[8] When applying design thinking, it can be startling to learn how certain systems, processes, and products were designed for "ease" over "value" to end users. For instance, just ask yourself, why is a vending machine designed to require you to bend down, reach your hand into a hole, and pick up your candy bar? Why not just design the vending machine to hand it directly to you? IDEO was able to raise these types of questions because they spent time watching and analyzing how end users interacted with vending machines.[9] Gravity made the design and engineering processes easier on the back end but more troublesome for consumers like you and me! Just imagine what your legal team could do by spending time observing your own interactions, objectively of course, with your clients!

9. **Implement low-investment, high-impact initiatives.** This strategy is just as it sounds. Identify solutions or initiatives that require low investments in time, finances, and human capital, but yield high impacts to your organization, team, constituents or beneficiaries. This is a strategy that I picked up in the nonprofit sector, a world that is forced to be creative due to a variety of limited resources. Low-investment, high-impact initiatives can also direct you to the most practical path forward, as some brainstorming sessions can lead to wonderful ideas that are unfortunately too complex or costly to implement…leading to a gridlock in action. Find what works and move the baton forward.

10. **Think like an entrepreneur.** If you are at a larger organization (e.g., biglaw), you may find yourself in a reactive position. Work will naturally flow your way and you have to deal with managing a firehose of tasks and putting out fires. Alternatively, if you are at a smaller organization, you need to be more proactive in your day-to-day as you'll receive fewer unsolicited queries for business, you'll have fewer recurring matters, and you'll need to build out and expand your organization. Ben Horowitz provides a brilliant analysis of this distinction between proactive and reactive work roles in *A Hard Thing About Hard Things*, one of my favorite books on the reality of running a business.[10] Although this strategy

is most applicable to attorneys at larger firms, as attorneys at smaller firms are, by nature, required to be more entrepreneurial (or else they won't get paid), the principles discussed can still benefit all attorneys in structuring their creative mindset. After all, there's a reason why the greatest entrepreneurs are constantly reading and constantly learning – entrepreneurship is about continuous growth and improvement, not about static positioning. By adopting an entrepreneurial mindset, you can make ideation a core principle of your practice so that you proactively look for opportunities to improve, whether to increase your legal skillset or to increase your business pipeline.

11. **Act.** This is the most important part of creative thinking and creative problem-solving. Ideation means nothing without action. Learning means nothing without action. Putting things into motion is the critical and most difficult step of creativity. It can be easy to come up with ideas, but it is extremely difficult to come up with actionable ideas. Throw in practical constraints like budgeting and the pool of ideas grows even smaller. But limitations are often a breeding ground for new and even more creative ideas. To create actionable solutions, especially within a firm setting, it can help to create a business plan that details: the problem or opportunity, the solution, specific action items, the projected costs, the projected resources required, supporting research as applicable, and an estimated timeline for execution. As many organizations have strict budgets designated for various causes, having a clear plan and understanding of the expense output will help translate your ideas into action at budget committee meetings. Having a clear plan will also help generate buy-in from key decision makers and keep the team organized, focused, and efficient throughout implementation process.

As you work your way through these strategies, you may begin to notice synergies and overlaps. These strategies are meant to be combined, intermixed, and interplayed. For example, you may choose to build a diverse team to embrace interdisciplinary thinking in efforts to identify your organization's pressure points and develop a low-investment, high-impact solution.

Applying these creative problem-solving methods in practice requires navigating the organizational structures and formalities of your team. This may require you to loop in and pitch your ideas to decision makers, prepare proposals and presentations for budgeting committees, revise your proposals with committee feedback, and finalize your proposal for approval or rejection (see Sections 3.2 and 9.1 for additional details on what to include in these proposals). An approach that I've found helpful is to frame the new initiative as a "pilot program" or a "pilot initiative." This will help reduce the psychological cost of venturing into new territory and increase your chances of getting your initiative approved.

Additionally, teamwork can be a large part of applying these creative strategies. This may involve collaborating with colleagues from different groups or practices. These cross-team collaborations can be helpful for two primary reasons: (i) different views and skillsets can help you develop a more holistic action plan, which will improve your overall execution, and (ii) working across teams can help you split or even increase your budget.

I like to think that creative problem solving is a little like mixed martial arts: there are a few core fundamentals that everyone needs to know like boxing and grappling, but you get to build your art form by adapting styles that work for you while discarding others. And like mixed martial arts, you can build your confidence through repeated successes, regardless of how small or large. In psychology, this is commonly referred to as self-efficacy, which I discuss further in Section 13.2.

I look forward to starting this creative journey with you. Let's connect ideas, concepts, and solutions together in unique and impactful ways. Think well, my friends.

PART II: THE CREATIVITY PLAYBOOK

§3
Question The Status Quo

Best practices do not equal prior practice.

§3.1: Overview

As we previously discussed in the opening sections, legal precedence holds a special place in our common law system in the United States. But the principle of legal precedence should not spill over into the business of law. In legal practice, best practices too often equal prior practices, a concept that I will refer to as the "Best Practice Dilemma." Attorneys tend to be more risk averse than the general population and they tend to find comfort in reliability and predictability. Because going against the grain would require attorneys to deviate from their personal, professional, and psychological preferences, prior practices tend to stay past their sell-by-dates.

Attorneys aren't trained to seek new and better ways of doing things throughout their careers, and it isn't until they assume leadership roles that they begin to think about the business of law. Unfortunately, this is too late. It's like being up for partner and realizing that business development is integral to your success as an attorney. Relationships take years to build and nourish. They don't happen overnight. And too often do I hear junior partners and attorneys up for partnership discuss how they wish they thought about business development earlier. The fix is simple: provide business development training and opportunities to junior attorneys. This ensures that attorneys are thinking about bringing in clients from day one. Then, when they become more senior, they would have years of relationships and experiences to draw on. To those that argue that investing in business development training on junior attorneys doesn't yield a high return on investment because the retention rate of junior to senior attorneys is low, I would encourage you to consider the following wisdom from Sir Richard Branson, the CEO and founder of the Virgin Group: "Train people well enough so they can leave, treat them well enough so they don't want to."[11] A large percentage of attorneys leave their organizations or teams because of the people they work with or for. It naturally follows that treating your attorneys well will increase your retention rates and help you recoup your training investment.

One of the best methods to counteract the Best Practice Dilemma and drive creative thinking is to question the status quo. This is one of the most fundamental strategies for innovation and creativity. But knowing something in theory and putting that something into practice are completely different animals. When was the last time you questioned the status quo? And, if you did question the norm, did you do anything about it? By way of analogy, knowing that you should exercise every day is very different than actually accomplishing it.

When clients are exploding your inbox at all hours of the day, it can be difficult to find time to ask yourself whether things could be done in more efficient or effective ways. In the eleventh hour, it's important to just get the tasks done based on what worked in the past because it was reliable. And, it's also possible to think that "it's someone else's job" to find better ways of doing things. But rather than thinking about all the reasons against challenging the status quo, let's think about all the reasons why we should.

As a baseline, challenging the status quo requires you to first understand that status quo. This requires you to take a step back and take stock of your present situation – e.g., the equivalent of the diligence or the document review stage. Start by observing your practices and the practices of your team. Then, start to widen your scope to see if there are any analogous lessons that you can learn by speaking with colleagues in different departments. The tax group may handle their client alerts very differently than the venture capital group. When you are conducting your diligence, be sure to speak with people where appropriate, including the staff. The more people you hear from, the more holistic of a picture you can create for yourself. This fact-gathering process can help you become a more informed attorney – you studied case law in law school, but did you ever study law firms and legal teams?

Once you've taken some time to analyze existing practices, begin to question why certain processes and procedures are the way they are. Are there certain practices that can be and should be improved? Are there certain practices that should be delegated to specialists that aren't? Is the opposite true? Are there certain tasks that should be delegated to administrators but aren't? On the flipside, while good practices should be continued, they shouldn't escape your radar. If a certain practice is good, can it be better? Your organization may have a great diversity and inclusion platform, but can it be improved to provide specific skills-based training to certain groups in addition to the existing offerings like programs that foster cultural awareness, mentorship, and social collegiality?

For example, something as basic as a client alert could be transformed into something more impactful. As it stands, client alerts are typically shared through firm websites, social media postings, and attorney advertising emails. What if we took a moment to ask ourselves whether the age-old client alert could be improved? I was speaking with Mahnu Davar, a partner at Arnold & Porter Kaye Scholer LLP in Washington, D.C., and he shared with me a brilliantly simple, yet powerful idea that he received after speaking with some of his technology clients: create a client alert podcast. By transforming the medium of how client alerts are transmitted, firms can provide their insights on legal trends in a manner that better conforms to client preferences (e.g., listening to a podcast during a morning commute or workout). By questioning the status quo of something as banal as a client alert, you can find a value-generating initiative for your clients and your team.[12]

To make questioning the status quo more accessible, we can leverage the power of counterfactual thinking, which is the process by which we imagine how particular events could have turned out differently. We, in fact, do this quite often after we suffer the negative consequences of a particular action or inaction. *If I didn't binge watch Netflix last night, I wouldn't have overslept and missed my meeting. If I had studied more, I would've done better. If I wasn't texting, I would've avoided the accident.* In these examples, we visualize alternate universes where the events unfolded differently. But, we can leverage this mode of thinking by flipping the script and focusing forward instead of backwards. By shifting our focus forward and asking "what if," we can start to train ourselves to think about what could be rather than what could have been. We can start to imagine how the status quo can be changed. We can start to think creatively and innovatively. Rather than thinking "if I had more time to diligence these documents, I would have been able to develop a more robust work product in the time given," you can focus forward and think "what if I could automate the diligence review of low-hanging fruit by using artificial intelligence to cover more ground in the same amount of time?" This would reserve your focus and time on more complex documents with the simple documents analyzed with diligence software. If you amd your team still aren't on board with the use of artificial intelligence, think about how you rely on Westlaw or Lexis to rank your most viable hits. You, too, are relying on software to provide you with certain information; however, this process has been established as the status quo for conducting case law research. You've been trained to scrutinize the results and "Shepardize" to ensure that you find the most relevant cases. Although initial searches may not be perfect, it's highly more efficient than searching through the dusty pages of reporters hidden in the corner of a law library. The same is true of artificial intelligence. It's meant to be a tool to help facilitate research, but it's up to the individual to scrutinize the results. One tool has been accepted while the other hasn't.

By asking "what if," you can be ahead of the curve. Just like how we can't imagine a world without Westlaw or Lexis, we will one day be unable to imagine a world without artificial intelligence.

For clarity, not all counterfactual questions have to be as grand as applying emerging technology to your business of practice; it can be as simple as asking whether your client alerts can be presented differently to your clients or whether entering in your time can be streamlined.

Attorneys have the unique ability to ask deep, enlightening questions of their clients. This skill translates naturally over to asking questions about the business of your organization or team. By focusing this ability inward rather than outwards (to a client), attorneys can become adept at improving the very institutions they make up. All this requires is re-imagining yourself, your firm, and your team as the client. So, I ask this of you: *what would you advise, counselor?*

§3.2: Application

Questioning the status quo is a continuous process, not a static event. It, like the other creative problem-solving methods, requires habit formation and repetition. It also requires support from team members across the organization, both horizontally and vertically.

With this understanding in mind, let's take a look at how this strategy can be applied in practice. Note that this application section serves as a guide. Depending on your situation, certain steps may or may not be applicable and other steps may be required.

Questioning The Status Quo: Organizational Level

Step 1: Conduct due diligence on the practice you are looking to improve. This includes speaking with colleagues, as appropriate.

Step 2: Ask yourself how this practice can be improved or different (i.e., what if?). Work to generate between five to ten ideas and then shortlist your ideas in order of practicality and difficulty.

Step 3: Socialize your shortlist of ideas with your peers and colleagues to get a sense of interest and to source feedback.

Step 4: Incorporate the feedback and revise the order of your shortlist as necessary (e.g., is something more challenging than you initially expected?).

Step 5: From your shortlist, select the idea(s) that you would like to pursue. Develop a short, one to two paragraph proposal for implementing each of these ideas. A proposal will help provide key information for decision makers and should identify, at a minimum: (i) the opportunity, (ii) a high-level action plan detailing the potential solution, (iii) background research (as applicable), (iv) resources required, and (v) implementation timeline. This proposal will be helpful in the next step.

Step 6: Reach out to the decision makers to discuss your idea(s) over a conversation, noting that you have a short proposal that you can share (this shows that you are prepared, but don't send this unless it's requested). Be prepared to "pitch" your idea and discuss the items you included in your proposal. Be prepared to address counterarguments and concerns as well. Remember, challenging the status quo means challenging the accepted practice, and certain decision makers may be partial to "the way things have always been done." It's your job to explain why things can be even better for the organization with your idea(s). At the end of your discussion, offer to send over your proposal with any updates from your conversation.

Step 7: The decision maker may need to submit your information to a committee for approval or spend some more time analyzing your proposal. Be patient. If you don't hear back in one to two weeks, follow up gently.

Step 8: If you get the green light, act. Pull together a team, if needed and approved, and begin to lay down an action plan for execution. Creativity is more than just ideation, it's about being able to materialize that idea into reality. If you don't get the green light, return to the drawing board to either revise your proposal or put on the breaks. Not all ideas succeed on their first attempt, or second, or third. If you believe that your idea will improve the workplace, continue pursuing it. Alternatively, if an idea is dead, return to the other items on your shortlist or go back to the drawing board altogether. Creativity is a process – not a one-time act.

Other Considerations: The creative process is rarely linear and you may have to repeat certain of the above steps multiple times or take detours that weren't mentioned. You may also end up skipping steps. If this happens, lean in. Navigating the process will lead to personal and professional growth, regardless of whether your idea proceeds forward or not.

One approach that you can take in questioning the status quo is to isolate one major initiative and break that down into phases: short term, medium term, and long term. If you are looking to build out a new practice area, for instance, this would require bringing on lateral attorneys with deep experience in the field, strengthening your team's reputation in that area, driving new business, and establishing a new talent pipeline. All at once, this can seem like an overwhelming task. But, by breaking things down into phases, implementation becomes much more manageable.

Another consideration is to factor in where your firm, organization, or team is in its lifecycle. If you are a new business, you'll be testing out new ideas on a weekly, if not daily, basis. If you've been around for a few years and are looking to expand, be mindful that your status quo may be naturally evolving in response to growth and that certain issues may not be top priorities (e.g., increasing dining budgets for summer programs). Or, if you are in biglaw, firm-wide structural changes will be more difficult to implement unless you are on the leadership team; however, office-wide or practice-group specific ideas may be of immediate value.

If you are struggling to get buy-in on a particular initiative, try proposing a pilot initiative to test out its viability and impact. This lessens the psychological weight of pursuing something new and different. It's also more difficult for someone to say no to a "test" than the implementation of a full-on initiative.

Lastly, always be respectful. To your juniors, to your peers, to your seniors. Creative problem solving is a collective process, no one needs to feel marginalized or isolated.

Questioning The Status Quo: Individual Level

Step 1: Conduct due diligence on a particular practice of yours that you are looking to improve.

Step 2: Ask yourself how your practice can be improved or different (i.e., what if?). Work to generate between five to ten ideas and then shortlist your ideas in order of practicality and difficulty.

Step 3: Socialize your shortlist of ideas with your peers and colleagues to get a sense of interest and to source feedback.

Step 4: Incorporate the feedback and revise the order of your shortlist as necessary (e.g., is something more challenging than you initially expected?).

Step 5: Act. You don't need approval or buy-in from decision makers to improve your status quo. Perhaps you realized that your soft skills are not up to par and you want to work on strengthening your verbal communication skills. You decide to source information and best practices from free online resources and practice speaking with your friends. Take that first step and start. Getting the ball rolling is the hardest part, but once you build up that momentum, you will be amazed by how quickly you can improve your status quo.

Other Considerations: Questioning our personal status quo can be difficult at first because it requires us to be vulnerable. For instance, we tend to overestimate our abilities in areas that we aren't experts in (here, the business of legal practice) due to a principle known as illusory superiority and coming to terms with this realization can be a humbling experience.[13] It is, however, necessary to help us paint an accurate picture of our abilities. This can help us better assess our strategies and approaches and it can also help us identify areas that we can creatively supplement and improve. I like to believe that we are all working to become better, and challenging your status quo is an effective means of ensuring that you are focusing on the right areas to improve – areas that you may not have considered without turning your view inwards.

§4
Identify Pressure Points

A good idea is like medicine, it takes away the pain.

§4.1: Overview

Pressure points are those areas of weakness, frustration, or pain. When generating ideas, a helpful tactic is to identify an organization's pressure points and ideate solutions to alleviate such pressure. Pressure points are present in every person, team, and organization, and taking the time to develop solutions can: (i) save a sinking ship, (ii) reinforce the fort, or (iii) drive innovation. In the first scenario, an organization may be bleeding money because it was carrying too much excess weight (e.g., non-productive business lines). Solving this challenge by spinning off or terminating such business lines could give the business a fighting chance. In the second scenario, an organization may be well positioned in the market and even the market leader. But, in efforts to strengthen the business, the organization decides to invest in upgrading its cybersecurity practices to provide additional assurances to its clients. This move, especially in light of increased exposure to cyberattacks globally, can strengthen the overall integrity of the organization by reinforcing an area of potential exposure. Lastly, in the third scenario, identifying an organization's pressure points can help drive innovation. Perhaps you realize that your legal team is finding it difficult to scale your practice even though you have the expertise and experience to take on larger clients. Rather than maintaining the status quo (yes, these strategies are all interlinked), you decide to address this pressure point head on by being innovative and leaning into legal technology: you adapt a new CRM platform to better manage your business development pipeline and stay on top of your prospects. By reducing this administrative burden from your team and staff, they can better focus on getting in front of prospects at the right time with the right information.

In perhaps more familiar terms, identifying pressure points is much like issue spotting in a given fact pattern. The only difference is that you are spotting business issues rather than legal issues and the given fact pattern is that of your organization, team, or yourself rather than that of a client's. In this way, attorneys are already trained to apply a critical eye towards a particular situation or set of circumstances. Refocusing this training can help attorneys strengthen their teams and themselves.

§4.2: Application

Identifying pressure points is a bit more delicate than some of the other creative problem-solving strategies from this playbook because these areas are likely hidden from view. It may require you to do some digging. If you are a junior attorney, your senior attorneys may not disclose these pressure points to you because they don't directly affect your job description. As a first-year associate, for instance, you may not be as familiar with how much business is derived from recurring clients versus new business or what percentage of business is derived from a single or small group of clients. On the flipside, if you are a senior attorney, you may be more aware of certain firm-wide or team-wide pressure points, but less aware of pressure points on the ground. For instance, a partner may not be as aware of issues at the junior levels because certain information may be difficult to communicate upwards. Is there a mid-level or senior associate that manages up well (e.g., plays nice with the partners) but manages down poorly (e.g., shifts blame and responsibility to juniors, abuses power, blocks opportunities to juniors)? The junior attorneys may not feel comfortable voicing their experiences to the partners especially if the mid-level or senior associate in question is valuable to the firm, which then becomes an issue of tolerating bad behavior at the workplace. Both perspectives, that of the junior and the senior attorneys, provide valuable insights into different aspects of the firm and each perspective is a product of the attorneys' respective positions within the organization or team. Thus, regardless of your level of seniority, taking the time to fact gather can lead you to uncover key pressure points to ideate around.

Let's take a look at how this strategy can be applied in practice. Note that this application section serves as a guide. Depending on your situation, certain steps may or may not be applicable and other steps may be required.

Identifying Pressure Points: Organizational Level

Step 1: Conduct due diligence on your team or organization. This includes speaking with colleagues, as appropriate. Think about potential areas of weakness, frustration, or pain. When you apply pressure to an area of your business, what gives way?

Often, people are already aware of certain pressure points because everyone complains about them. These items are the low-hanging fruit. The question is, has anyone tried to act on it and fix the problem? Here's your opportunity to make a difference.

One method of identifying these areas is to imagine yourself as a competitor. *How would you compete against your team or yourself? What weaknesses would you capitalize on to gain market share and where would you apply pressure?*

Relatedly, try imaging yourself as the CEO (or the CEO equivalent like the managing partner, executive director, or general counsel). *What areas of your business do you need to reinforce or improve? Are there areas where your competitors are outcompeting you? If so, why? Do your attorneys need more support in a particular area? What happens to the business infrastructure when it gets busy? What happens to the business infrastructure when it's quiet?*

Another method of isolating these areas is to undergo the SWOT analysis, which focuses on identifying an organization's strengths, weaknesses, opportunities, and threats.[14] Although there are multiple variations of this analysis, the fundamental 2x2 matrix on the next page has withstood the test of time and remains an invaluable tool for business leaders and strategists.

Going through the SWOT analysis can help you categorize the information you are gathering. The right column (Weaknesses, Threats) represent pressure points. The left column (Strengths, Opportunities) can help you contextualize your pressure points and also serve as a tool for you to generate additional creative ideas. See Section 12 to see how the SWOT analysis fits into the strategy of thinking like a founder/entrepreneur.

Step 2: Work to generate between five to ten ideas to resolve your identified pressure point(s) and then shortlist your ideas in order of practicality and difficulty.

For example, if you are looking to improve your firm's diversity and inclusion efforts, internal programming, without more, is not enough. It can help to get involved with nonprofit organizations and diverse bar associations to directly engage with your community.

SWOT

Strengths (Internal)	Weaknesses (Internal)
Identify areas that your organization excels at. Think about your competitive advantages, including your brand, clients, and your attorneys and staff (all important factors for legal practice).	Identify areas that your organization needs to improve. Think about inhibitors or areas that are causing a loss in value, including high attrition rates, lack of diversity, lack of leadership, and employee happiness (all areas that can be improved in legal practice generally).
Opportunities (External)	**Threats (External)**
Identify areas outside of your organization that can give you a competitive advantage. Think about the external forces that you can capitalize on, including increased market demand for your particular services (e.g., cybersecurity).	Identify areas outside of your organization that can be harmful to your business. Think about the external forces that can lead to a dent in your bottom line, including increased opportunities for attorneys outside of practice and commoditization of your services.

Step 3: Socialize your shortlist of ideas with your peers and colleagues to get a sense of interest and to source feedback.

Step 4: Incorporate the feedback and revise the order of your shortlist as necessary (e.g., is something more challenging than you initially expected?).

Step 5: From your shortlist, select the idea(s) that you would like to pursue. Develop a short, one to two paragraph proposal for implementing each of these ideas. A proposal will help provide key information for decision makers and should identify, at a minimum: (i) the opportunity, (ii) a high-level action plan, (iii) background research (as applicable), (iv) resources required, and (v) implementation timeline. This proposal will be helpful in the next step.

Step 6: Reach out to the decision makers to discuss your idea(s) over a conversation, noting that you have a short proposal that you can share (this shows that you are prepared, but don't send this unless it's requested). Be prepared to "pitch" your idea and discuss the items you included in your proposal. Be prepared to address counterarguments and concerns as well. Remember, identifying your organization's pressure points can put decision makers on the defensive. It's your job to explain how you can address these areas respectfully and constructively. At the end of your discussion, offer to send over your proposal with any updates from your conversation.

Step 7: The decision maker may need to submit your information to a committee for approval or spend some more time analyzing your proposal. Be patient. If you don't hear back in one to two weeks, follow up gently.

Step 8: If you get the green light, act. Pull together a team, if needed and approved, and begin to lay down an action plan for execution. Creativity is more than just about ideation, it's about being able to materialize that idea into reality. If you don't get the green light, return to the drawing board to either revise your proposal or put on the breaks. Not all ideas succeed on their first attempt...or second, or third. If you believe that your idea will improve the workplace, continue pursuing it. Alternatively, if an idea is dead, return to the other items on your shortlist or go back to the drawing board altogether. Creativity is a process – not a one-time act.

Other Considerations: The creative process is rarely linear and you may have to repeat certain of the above steps multiple times or take detours that weren't mentioned. You may also end up skipping steps. If this happens, lean in. Navigating the process will lead to personal and professional growth, regardless of whether your idea proceeds forward or not.

One approach that you can take in identifying pressure points is to isolate one major initiative and break that down into phases: short term, medium term, and long term. If you are looking to build out a new practice area to fill a service gap, for instance, this would require bringing on lateral attorneys with deep experience in the field, strengthening your team's reputation in that area, driving new business, and establishing a new talent pipeline. All at once, this can seem like an overwhelming task. But, by breaking things down into phases, implementation becomes much more manageable.

Another consideration is to factor in where your firm, organization, or team is in its lifecycle. If you are a new business, you'll have more pressure points because you are still working on building out your foundation – in which case, identifying pressure points may not be productive. If you've been around for a few years and are looking to expand, identifying pressure points can help you reinforce certain areas of your business and expand. Or, if you are in biglaw, addressing firm-wide structural challenges will be more difficult unless you are on the leadership team; however, addressing challenges within your office or practice group can be more manageable regardless of your seniority.

In practice, some of you may have been told, "Don't bring me problems, bring me solutions." Attorneys don't necessarily make the best managers as they haven't been trained in the art of management. But some have become quite adept at it. Bad managers will tell you the above statement verbatim. Full stop. Not very encouraging is it? It's also a statement of authority and, quite frankly, a power play. Problems should be resolved collaboratively. Good managers use a variation of the above: "If you have a problem, turn over every stone before coming to me and if you can't figure it out let's work on it together." Attorneys are busy. Their time is their money. But this is exactly why it's important to build efficient and supportive teams. I've heard both of the above statements. The first doesn't encourage anyone to raise problems. The second does. It just requires that you do your best to come up with potential solutions first so that you can have a more meaningful discussion. It's much more productive to brainstorm when you have conducted diligence. Thus, if you uncover certain pressure points that you think need to be resolved and that you determine is appropriate for you to raise, don't be afraid to start the discussion even if you don't have a solution – just show that you've done your homework. The exception is when the clock is ticking. If an immediate problem occurs, you may not have time to do your research. Escalate the problem quickly so that you can work together to solve it quickly (or mitigate the damages).

Additionally, don't let a bad manager deter you from finding ways to contribute to your team. Share your ideas with a trusted peer or colleague. Perhaps your peer has a good manager that you can both speak with. There will be some instances where you may need to raise something with your bad manager. If this is the case, stay firm and bring as much research as possible. The good thing about attorneys is that logic and reason are respected above all else (and sometimes to a fault). Just make sure your logic and reason are sound.

Lastly, always be respectful. To your juniors, to your peers, to your seniors. Creative problem solving is a collective process, no one needs to feel marginalized or isolated.

Identifying Pressure Points: Individual Perspective

Step 1: Conduct due diligence on yourself. Think about your potential areas of weakness. When you apply pressure, what gives way? *Do you struggle with deadlines or managing multiple tasks at once? Can your networking skills be improved?*

Step 2: Work to generate between five to ten ideas to resolve your identified pressure point(s) and then shortlist your ideas in order of practicality and difficulty.

For example, if you are struggling to manage multiple tasks at once, consider using a spreadsheet to manage all your action items, deadlines, and progress. Alternatively, you may want to try the simple yet effective method of making daily to-do lists with pen and paper. The act of physically writing items down and crossing them off (or checking them off) can help you stay more organized than using a to-do list app – similar to how writing down notes facilitates better understanding of new material than typing them down. Physically writing items down forces you to engage with the material in the physical world rather than the digital world.

Step 3: Socialize your ideas with trusted colleagues. Here, it's important to discuss this with people that are interested in your well-being and improvement because sharing these thoughts with the wrong people can be a strategic landmine. *Will implementing your ideas really improve your time management skills, workflow prioritization, responsiveness, or business development or will it make it more difficult? Is there something you are missing? Are there best practices and resources you weren't aware of?*

Step 4: Incorporate the feedback and revise the order of your shortlist if necessary (e.g., did you learn that focusing on strengthening a particular skill is more important than the other items on your list?).

Step 5: Act. You don't need approval or buy-in from decision makers to address your pressure points. Take that first step and start. Getting the ball rolling is the hardest part, but once you build up that momentum, you will be amazed by how quickly you can improve these areas so that they are no longer your pressure points. We are all working towards self-improvement; we are in this together.

Other Considerations: Similar to questioning the status quo from Section 3, identifying your personal pressure points can be difficult at first because it requires us to be vulnerable. For instance, we tend to overestimate our abilities in areas that we aren't experts in (here, the business of legal practice) due to a principle known as illusory superiority and coming to terms with the realization that we aren't as good as we think we are can be a humbling experience.[15] It is, however, necessary to help us paint an accurate picture of our abilities. This can help us better assess our strategies and approaches and it can also help us identify areas that we can creatively supplement and improve. I like to believe that we are all working to become better, and identifying your pressure points is an effective means of ensuring that you are focusing on the right areas to improve – areas that you may not have considered without turning your view inwards.

§5
Generate More Ideas

Success is a numbers game.

§5.1: Overview

A team encounters a problem and the members decide to hold a brainstorming session. They gather in a room or virtual environment, begin sharing their ideas, and write down potential solutions. After some time, the discussion starts to revolve around two or three ideas. From there, one of these is selected as the appropriate course of action. The idea flow ends. The session ends. And everyone calls it a day from the ideation standpoint.

If this sounds familiar to you, it's because we've all been there. This is how a brainstorming session typically occurs in a corporate setting; however, there are two main flaws with this approach: (i) brainstorming sessions are rarely guided, and (ii) the number of ideas is limited.

First, going through an unguided brainstorming session is like going to the gym without a trainer. You may get some benefits, but you aren't maximizing your time or potential. This first point is the focus of this playbook. Second, the number of ideas generated from a typical brainstorming session is limited to the low-hanging fruit. These are the "easy" ideas that almost any other similarly situated group would come up with. This leaves out an entire realm of possibilities: the unique ideas that can generate more value than the obvious ones. This second point is the focus of this section.

There are times when the obvious answer is the correct approach. But when the problem requires creativity, innovation, and differentiation, the obvious answer (at least in the initial instance – some solutions are incredibly obvious when we apply our hindsight vision but were incredibly difficult to come up with at the outset) may not be the best. To solve novel challenges, create differentiation, and drive change, new ideas must be crafted. When clients are monitoring fees more closely than ever, when legal services are becoming commoditized, when fee discounts are becoming standard practice, when diversity and inclusion is becoming more highly valued, when technology is beginning to disrupt legal practice, when attorney preferences are changing, prior practice does not equal best practice. By working to increase our ideas during the brainstorming stage, we can increase our optionality and work towards better solutions.

§5.2: Application

One of the most difficult aspects of creating new ideas and solutions is that it can feel like an uphill battle, especially in the law. People feel a certain level of comfort or safety in precedent and taking risks with new ideas isn't part of the job description...after all, attorneys are in the business of risk management and mitigation. But when it's your business, your practice, and your livelihood that's on the line, putting in the time and effort to make that uphill push can help position yourself and your team on the high ground. What has helped me in generating more ideas is to recognize my initial ideation wall. When I'm collaborating with a team and we toss around ideas, there's typically an inflection point of energy and enthusiasm. This is the ideation wall, similar to "the wall" that distance runners hit. The magic key to increasing your ideas is to fight past this wall to come up with one more idea. And then another. And then another. It can help to take a coffee break or resume discussions at a later time or date, time permitting of course. If you are under the gun, then it's time to dig deep.

The analogy in legal practice is ensuring that no stone is left unturned. We may find two or three cases or statutes that we believe are on point because they show up at the top of our Westlaw or Lexis search. But we are trained to not stop there. We are trained to go further. We are trained to check how the case or statutes have fared over time: how have they been interpreted, have they been supported, were they overturned, are there other cases or statutes that come into play? And we are trained to refine and revise our search terms. The same is true for brainstorming and ideation. It's a habit and it's a process, much like legal research and strategy.

Increasing the number of ideas that you come up with is a simple yet powerful tactic when it comes to creative problem solving. When going through this process, some ideas may come from left field while others originate from another universe entirely. Some ideas may result in strange permutations of good ideas and others may be terrible ones. And while your ninth idea may be garbage, your tenth idea may result in a gold mine. The process of generating more ideas expands your pool of ideas and, thus, your optionality. It stretches your imagination and challenges you to think more creatively. There is a term in sales called "prospecting," which describes the process of searching for and generating new business (e.g., the process of getting sales). This term is also apt for describing the goal of ideating: searching for the right idea. As you are prospecting for ideas, you will encounter far more bad ideas than good ones just as you would encounter more "no's" than "yes's" in sales. And just as in sales, ideating is a numbers game. It may take a hundred cold calls and ninety-nine rejections to generate one sale. The same is true when brainstorming.

A master salesperson knows, however, that a "no" today may translate into a "yes" tomorrow. So, this person will often keep detailed records of each encounter with a prospect in case a future opportunity arises. With brainstorming, it is also important to create a record of your ideas. Just because some ideas may not fit the situation today, doesn't mean it may not come into play moving forward…or, it may be a solution to a different problem that you are having. This is why so many successful entrepreneurs and business people have troves of jam-packed notebooks with diagrams next to scribbles next to numbers. And if you don't have a notebook on hand, your phone notetaking app can be a great clutch.

Let's take a look at how this strategy can be applied in practice. Note that this application section serves as a guide. Depending on your situation, certain steps may or may not be applicable and other steps may be required.

Generate More Ideas: Organizational Level

Step 1: Schedule your brainstorming session as you normally would.

Step 2: Begin your brainstorming process, whether by incorporating the creative problem-solving principles discussed in this playbook or others.

Step 3: Write down all of your ideas, regardless of how ridiculous they may sound at the outset.

Perhaps you are part of a team that is tasked with starting a new office in a new city for your firm and you are directly responsible for driving community relationships. At your initial brainstorming session, you might come up with the following ideas: (i) get involved with pro bono work, (ii) join local bar associations, and (iii) sponsor community events.

Or perhaps you are tasked with coming up with new events for your summer associate program. At your initial brainstorming session, you might come up with following ideas: (i) whiskey tasting, (ii) going on a boat cruise, and (iii) attending a concert.

Step 4: At a certain point, the ideation train begins to slow. If you are not under a time crunch, take a break or schedule another meeting. This can help jumpstart your mind so that you can begin another brainstorming session with a fresh and clear perspective. Once you regroup, work on coming up with at least one to two more ideas.

If you are under the gun, you will have to grind and work through this ideation wall. Take five minutes to grab coffee, take a quick shower, grab a snack, or take a short walk. Reset. And proceed forward. Challenge yourself to come up with at least one to two more ideas.

In the new office example, you may not have come up with the following ideas if you had stopped at your ideation wall: (i) developing a talent pipeline by sponsoring high school and law school students to pursue careers in law, and (ii) creating a fellowship for graduating law students to pursue work in the public interest sector.

In the summer program example, you may not have come up with the following ideas if you had stopped at your ideation wall: (i) hosting an indoor skydiving event, or (ii) hosting an event at a trapeze school.

Following Step 4, you will have successfully taken the first step to generating more ideas. Remember, those one to two more ideas are exponentially more difficult to come up with because they aren't the low-hanging fruit. These ideas may be fruitful or they may not. But it's worth the effort because the potential upside (e.g., better initiatives) outweighs the potential downside (e.g., scheduling one extra meeting to generate a few more possibilities).

Step 5: To the extent relevant, share your ideas with your peers or with your broader team. This will help you refine and pressure test your ideas.

Step 6: Act. Ideas only have value when they are acted upon. Don't let your ideas sit in the dark, but work hard to bring them to light regardless of how hard that may be.

Step 7: Repeat these steps in your future brainstorming sessions and meetings. Generating one to two more ideas beyond what you would normally do is the first step. Work to triple or even quadruple your ideas. Over time, you'll be able to develop this into a habit.

Considerations: Simply getting into the mindset of trying to come up with more ideas will help you think more creatively. Embrace this process because it can be rewarding, help you stand out, and, quite simply, be fun. Collaborating and generating ideas is an act of creating something from nothing. It's the first step.

When going through this process, it can become difficult to gauge the quality of the ideas that you are coming up with. Keeping your end goal in mind can help: to generate more ideas to create more optionality and value for your team. Coming up with more ideas, even if outlandish, doesn't mean coming up with hollow ideas. It means creating ideas with integrity, even if some ideas may not initially fit any particular schema.

Generating More Ideas: Individual Level

Step 1: Schedule your personal brainstorming session as you normally would. This may be the time you take for yourself to think and reflect, such as during your commute, during your workouts, or during your meals. It doesn't have to be anything formal.

Step 2: Begin your brainstorming process, whether by incorporating the creative problem-solving principles discussed in this playbook or others.

Step 3: Write down all of your ideas, regardless of how ridiculous they may sound at the outset.

You may be looking for more ways to get sharpen your lawyering skills. At your brainstorming session, you may come up with the following: (i) work harder, (ii) get staffed on more deals or cases (e.g., work harder), and (iii) take on more pro bono cases (e.g., work even harder).

Step 4: At a certain point, the ideation train begins to slow. If you are not under a time crunch, take a break or pick this up at a later time. This can help jumpstart your mind so that you can begin another brainstorming session with a fresh and clear perspective. Once you start up the process again, work on coming up with at least one to two more ideas.

If you are under the gun, you will have to grind and work through this ideation wall. Take five minutes to grab coffee, take a quick shower, grab a snack, or take a short walk. Reset. And proceed forward. Challenge yourself to come up with at least one to two more ideas.

After pushing through the wall and resetting, you work on thinking of a few additional ideas: (i) join a board to put yourself in the shoes of your clients as a decision maker (e.g., work smarter), and (ii) explore different fields to source best practices like applying business principles to your practice to increase your efficiency or become a better manager (e.g., work smarter).

Following Step 4, you will have successfully taken the first step to generating more ideas. Remember, those one to two more ideas are exponentially more difficult to come up with because they aren't the low-hanging fruit. These ideas may be fruitful or they may not. But the potential upside of finding that great idea is worth the extra effort and time investment.

Step 5: To the extent relevant, share your ideas with your peers or with your broader team. This will help you refine and pressure test your ideas. Sharing these ideas in the context of your goals can also help inform your network that you may be interested in certain opportunities like taking on community roles. You never know, they may be in a position to help.

Step 6: Act. Ideas only have value when they are acted upon. Don't let your ideas sit in the dark, but work hard to bring them to light regardless of how hard it is.

Step 7: Repeat these steps in your future brainstorming sessions and meetings. Generating one to two more ideas beyond what you would normally do is the first step. The goal is to increase ideation by a magnitude of three.[16] Over time, you'll be able to develop this into a habit.

Considerations: Have fun with this process. Coming up with more ideas is a challenge and you can see how each new idea you come up with is slightly more creative than the one that preceded it. By creating a larger idea pool, you can increase your optionality and expand your opportunities. Often times, especially for attorneys, it can be hard to think of ideas outside of the law. For instance, if you are thinking about making a career pivot, I often hear people say that they are stuck within their field and that they can only go in the government, academia, or in-house at a company. Candidly, if that's your field of view, those will be your only opportunities. But, if you look outside of legal practice, you'll start to see that attorneys have also made successful entrepreneurs (e.g., David Rubenstein, Peter Thiel), business leaders (e.g., Lloyd Blankfein), musicians (e.g., Andrea

Bocelli), and authors (e.g., John Grisham).[17]

§6
Develop Diverse Teams

Our differences are our strengths.

§6.1: Overview

Numerous studies have shown that team diversity increases effectiveness, productivity, and performance. This holds true in small group settings all the way up to corporate boards.[18] In fact, a study conducted by the Boston Consulting Group found that companies with more diverse management teams had 19% higher revenues than less diverse management teams due to innovation.[19] The hard part is figuring out how to build these teams in your organizations. It takes time. It takes money. It takes effort. It takes influence. And, most importantly, it takes a champion. Without someone taking point and leading, teams will remain dangerously and uncreatively homogenous.

To begin, developing an appropriate definition of diversity with your team is critical. Diversity is an inclusive term that captures race, ethnicity, culture, gender, age, experience, skill, thought, accessibility, and more. Inclusion is the natural corollary. Having a diverse team must also require that those diverse individuals are included at the table. If they aren't part of the decision-making process, aren't included in meetings, or their voices aren't heard, diversity is nothing more than a façade. We need inclusion.

A prime example of applying team diversity towards problem solving is through design thinking. This is a six-step process that is premised upon having a team of diverse individuals. The creative consulting firm IDEO is the prototype. You may find a biochemist, banker, designer, and philosopher working on the same IDEO team to solve a discrete business problem. More on design thinking in Section 10.

Another powerful example of promoting team diversity is California's statute that requires California-based companies to have at least one female director on their boards. By the end of 2021, these companies may be required to have at least two directors depending on their size.[20] Relatedly, proxy advisory firms like ISS and Glass Lewis are also supporting initiatives to drive team diversity by, for instance, voting against nominating committee chairs of boards with no female directors.[21]

In the legal sector, clients are now heavily pushing law firms to have at least one diverse attorney on their advisory team. Some companies are providing diversity bonuses to firms that exceed certain diversity metrics while other companies aren't hiring firms that are below average on diversity measures.[22] These are all powerful motivators for law firms to become more diverse; however, in my view, I believe that the intrinsic value of driving diversity should play a larger role. Law firms shouldn't have to wait for their clients to drive change because of financial incentives. They should take leadership and drive change on their own accord. They need to be proactive rather than reactive. For diversity initiatives to succeed, we need champions at every level of an organization contributing and leading the charge. Diversity is fundamental to the future success of any organization, and it's time to light that fire in the legal field.

§6.2: Application

Conceptually, it's not difficult to get on board with promoting diversity. It is, however, a challenge to effect diversity in practice. It requires a complex combination of short-term, mid-term, and long-term action items. To create more diverse teams, champions at all levels of an organization must be involved. If the drive comes exclusively from the top, there won't be a cultural shift and inclusion won't occur. Relatedly, if the drive comes exclusively from the bottom, institutional change won't be effected and inclusion won't occur. And if we exclude the middle of the organization, we leave out valuable leaders that can help lead and broker change from the top down and from the bottom up. Thus, if you are committed to driving diversity within your team and organization, become a champion and lead initiatives within the firm and in the community. If you don't consider yourself diverse, you can still become a champion by being an ally and an advocate.

In practice, this means that firms and organizations need to encourage attorneys at all levels of seniority to rise to the challenge. If you are a junior attorney, voice your commitment to diversity and play your part in supporting the diversity and inclusion team. If there isn't one, work with senior members to start one. If you are a senior attorney, work to include junior and mid-level attorneys on your team. Ideas should be sourced from all corners of your team and more junior attorneys can play a vital role in implementing certain initiatives. First-year attorneys can also bring a fresh energy and perspective to your diversity and inclusion practices because they can apply their recent law school experiences – which tend to be more forward looking than traditional firm practices. If you are a mid-level attorney, you are well positioned to connect driven junior attorneys with supportive senior attorneys. With your experience at the firm or organization, you can more easily take up leadership roles and mentor junior attorneys.

Depending on whether you are part of a small firm, mid-sized firm, biglaw firm, in-house team, governmental agency, nonprofit, or other organization, your approach to building diverse teams will vary. Investing millions into developing a diverse talent pipeline through sponsorships, scholarships, and programming may not be the most viable option if you are a firm of four attorneys. At the same time, a small firm may be able to more quickly drive organizational diversity due to a few key recruiting initiatives – for instance, a few classes of diverse attorneys can materially impact the culture and dynamic of a small team. While there isn't a one-size-fits-all solution, there is the collective problem of increasing diversity in the law. Firms and organizations can look to their peers and clients to get a sense of which practices work well and which ones don't. They can also look towards their clients or firms and organizations that are outside of their peer group. One best practice that is quickly emerging is the creation of new senior diversity roles like chief diversity officers. Another is the creation of diversity pipelines towards partnership.

While racial, ethnic, cultural, and gender diversity are in the spotlight, it's also important to remember that the definition of diversity is broader. Diversity of skill, thought, accessibility, disability, and experiences – along with others factors – are also instrumental in building diverse teams. For example, a team of litigators or a team of transactional attorneys with the same pedigree of experiences and skills will limit the number and types of ideas that can be developed. If your litigation team is full of former clerks and former government attorneys, hiring another attorney with that same background may not have as large of an impact on the team as compared to hiring a litigator that was formerly a management consultant or banker.

There has been considerable progress in the diversity and inclusion space over the past few years. Conversations around diversity are finally becoming mainstream and participating in these discussions can continue to expand our understanding of the intricacies behind the topic. For example, I recently had the pleasure of hosting a panel on diversity in the law and we had the privilege of hearing from a wide range of diverse attorneys, including a former general counsel who is completely blind. Not only was his story inspiring and humbling, but it was incredibly illuminating. It taught me about the highly important yet often forgotten category of accessibility.

As with many problem-solving strategies, building diverse teams can be paired with other approaches to drive creative thinking. Whenever you are engaging in team work, consider the potential benefits and bringing together individuals with a diverse set of skills, experiences, and backgrounds.

Let's take a look at how this strategy can be applied in practice. Note that this application section serves as a guide. Depending on your situation, certain steps may or may not be applicable and other steps may be required.

Building Diverse Teams

Step 1: At the beginning of a new project, assignment, or initiative, think about what type of team you are looking to build with your key stakeholders or core team.

Are you expanding a practice group? Are you expanding your entire legal team? Are you opening a new office? Are you staffing a new case or deal? Are you building a new team for an internal initiative (e.g., staff, firm citizenship, knowledge management, diversity and inclusion, training)?

Step 2: Spend some time objectively analyzing where your team or organization stands from a diversity standpoint. This may be a difficult discussion, but it's an important one. Having a strong, unbiased view of your current positioning is critical in helping you develop the right approach to drive more diverse teams.

Are you overly homogeneous? Are you ahead of the curve and are looking to do more? Do you have the appropriate resources to support you?

Depending on where you fall on the spectrum, you may have more or less latitude to drive diversity on your team.

Step 3: Based on your responses to Step 1 and Step 2, identify what types of diversity you wish to promote and determine what objective benchmarks you will use to track your progress. Looking towards industry norms can be a helpful first step, but, as these norms are typically behind the curve, they may be better served as initial benchmarks towards your end goal.

Are you focused on promoting gender equity in your firm? Are you looking to drive greater cultural, ethnic, and racial diversity on your team? Are you looking to bring on new skills to strengthen your team or fill knowledge gaps? Are you looking to better drive accessibility in your team? Or perhaps you are looking to drive all of the above.

Step 4: Based on your responses to Step 2 and Step 3, it may be helpful to expand your stakeholders or core team. It may be appropriate, for instance, to get the perspectives of more junior or senior attorneys. Promoting diversity isn't easy, and additional perspectives can be helpful. Additionally, for large scale initiatives, your team may wish to consider retaining outside advisors and consultants.

Step 5: Develop your action plan (i.e., an internal business plan) with your stakeholders or core team. Define your benchmarks, your goals, your purpose, the resources that you need, the projected timeline for implementation, and other components that you find helpful.

Step 6: Invite trusted colleagues outside of your stakeholders or core team to critique your action plan. This process can help you develop a more robust strategy.

Step 7: Incorporate any helpful feedback that you receive from Step 6 and revise your action plan as needed.

Step 8: If necessary, present your action plan to any required decision makers and revise as appropriate. A more detailed explanation of getting decision-maker approval can be found in Section 3.2, Questioning the Status Quo: Organizational Level, Steps 5-8.

Step 9: Act. Depending on where you are focused on driving diversity, your action plan may have a timeline of a few days, a few months, or a few years. Take that first step and begin shaping your team.

Step 10: After you've pulled together your diverse team or teams, it's important to leverage that diversity moving forward. Constructing the team is the first step. Putting them into action is the next. For example, if you are building a diverse practice group, host regular team meetings and collaborate. Encourage team members to share their ideas and experiences. Encourage team members to engage with the firm beyond their immediate practice area. To see how diverse teams can help you think apply interdisciplinary approaches, see Section 7.

Considerations: When strategizing over diversity initiatives, think about how to encourage a culture of diversity versus an instance of diversity. Cultural change can take time, but that's where the most value comes from. It can help to think of investing in diversity as investing in a long-term asset.

Popular strategies include: developing talent pipelines, establishing affinity groups (regardless of how small or big), supporting diversity initiatives in the firm and in the community, collaborating with other legal teams and firms on diversity initiatives, and providing mentorship.

An important point that tends to fly under the radar is how attorneys can benefit the team beyond his or her primary functionality as a legal advisor. Especially at larger firms, associates tend to be viewed only for what they can do to support their seniors – not what they can do for their team at large. Newly minted attorneys are incredibly talented. They not only survived law school, but they were heavily engaged and active with their law school communities and programs. They wrote for journal, they participated in pro bono projects, and they have a diverse range of skills. They should be engaged. If you are in a senior role, encourage your team members, including your juniors, to share their ideas on how to make your team or organization better (e.g., allow a certain amount of this time to count towards yearly billable requirements). This can help improve workplace morale by actively giving everyone a voice and empowering them to participate. If you are in a senior role and you only value your team members for what they can contribute to your clients, this can lead to attorneys feeling like hired guns or just another cog in the machine that can be replaced. It can be easy to forget that legal practice is a people business that includes both the interests of your clients and your team – your most valuable asset. Once you pull together your diverse team, empower them. The benefits will start trickling in. Most importantly, it's the right thing to do.

Relatedly, if you are a newer attorney, it's also important to think about how you can contribute to your team outside of your legal work. I understand the ambition to become the best attorney that you can be, but you don't have to put your blinders up and focus exclusively on legal work. You are more than what your profession defines you as. You have other skills, interests, and hobbies. It's important that you can bring your personality to work. You spend most of your waking hours at work or focusing on work. Creating and contributing to that work environment is important in helping you build a collaborative, supportive, and inclusive environment. Raise your hand. Get involved. And embrace your differences.

This is also an opportune time to discuss the concept of the "airport test" during interviews. *Is this candidate someone I would feel comfortable getting stuck with on a long layover for a business trip?*

This is an informal test that some attorneys employ when determining whether to hire a candidate or not – all things being equal. This kills diversity. People tend to hire people like themselves when this test is employed, which is why some legal teams are entirely homogeneous (e.g., same schools, same socio-economic upbringing, same backgrounds, etc.).

A better test is what I call the "fire drill test." When your case or deal is blowing up and it's 2 a.m., who do you want with you on your team? It doesn't matter if you both like the same football team or belong to the same country club. What does matter, however, is whether you are a reliable, loyal, and hardworking team player with the skillset necessary to support your team. Like the airport test, the fire drill test also factors in compatibility and likeability...or else you wouldn't want to work with them during a fire drill! The difference is that the emphasis is on what the candidate can bring to the table, not whether you have a coffee buddy when your flight is cancelled. Additionally, this person might not have been the most social in law school, but that person may have been the hardest working. Don't get me wrong, social skills are crucial for advising clients and business development. But those are qualities that can be trained. Being someone that strengthens your team, on the other hand, can't be.

§7
Embrace Interdisciplinary Thinking

Curiosity separates the known from the unknown.

§7.1: Overview

Interdisciplinary thinking is a keystone of creative problem solving. It can open up new worlds, spark novel solutions, and create more value for everyone. When we are stuck on a challenging problem, coming up with new ideas can be difficult. It can even feel like Groundhog Day when everyone keeps coming up with the same idea over and over again. To gain inspiration, looking towards a different field can help. It can give us the fresh perspective that we need to see the problem from a slightly different angle than before, which gives way towards developing a different, better solution. By learning from different fields, we can actually gain a deeper understanding of our prime discipline.[23]

A famous study by Michigan State University researchers found that scientists who won the Nobel Prize were significantly more likely to engage with the arts than scientists who didn't win the coveted prize. Specifically, Nobel Prize-winning scientists were 2x more likely to be involved in music, 7x more likely to be involved with art, 12x more likely to be involved with creative writing, and 22x more likely to be involved in the performing arts.[24] This pattern held true in a study of thousands of Americans who started their own business and applied for patent applications. These entrepreneurs and inventors were significantly more likely than their peers to have hobbies in the arts like painting, sculpture, and literature.[25] The interest and pursuit of new perspectives from differing disciplines, especially for hobbyists in the arts, can have a profound effect on your professional endeavors.

Engaging with different disciplines can also provide us with a needed mental break to help keep our minds fresh. This doesn't have to be complicated like getting a PhD. As noted in the studies above, this can be as simple as diving into your hobbies. Being focused on the same subject matter or item for too long is like driving down a long country road for hours on end: the monotony will get to you and you'll start to drift cognitively. By trying out that new cycling class, you can give yourself a nice mental break while learning something new.

For me, picking up new hobbies like rock climbing has helped me keep my mind and body fresh. Lawyers are notorious for throwing themselves into their work with little focus on their mental or physical health. But the healthier your mind and body, the better your work product and, most importantly, the happier you will be. Have you ever noticed how insanely successful entrepreneurs and CEOs devote time into their routines for self-care? It's because it works. When you recharge, you open up your mind for more creative thinking. It's also no surprise that we sometimes get our best ideas when we are doing something completely unrelated.

What I personally enjoy about rock climbing is that you can learn about your risk tolerance, improve your fitness, learn to calm your nerves, and have a little fun along the way. Rather than top-rope climbing or lead climbing, which both involve ropes and harnesses, I prefer bouldering because it is untethered. Bouldering occurs without ropes, on shorter climbing walls, and are designed to focus climbers on more complex "problems" (i.e., the arrangement of foot and hand holds on the wall). For me, the tangibility of falling paired with the goal of reaching the top heightens the process of decision making and risk taking, which I thoroughly enjoy. One wrong move and you can fall several feet towards the padded mats (which can still hurt). Overall, as a novice climber at best, bouldering has been a great way for me to introspect, disconnect, and refresh.

You can also learn a lot about others through rock climbing. Unlike some other sports, rock climbing comes with an inherent risk of injury. Your equipment can fail, you can fall the wrong way, or you can slam into the wall when trying to reach for your next hold. Watching how people respond when they are on the wall (especially bouldering without ropes) can be quite telling. Do they take risks? If they aren't sure whether they can reach the next hold, do they go for it or do they downclimb? How many times are they willing to try a problem over again if they can't complete it?

When diving into your curiosities, I always find it easier to engage with a subject or embark on an endeavor that you find enjoyable. If you do what you naturally gravitate towards, you'll always find a way to make it valuable. The same is true, I believe, for interdisciplinary thinking.

§7.2: Application

In practice, interdisciplinary thinking can take one of two different forms. First, as it's commonly understood, interdisciplinary thinking involves engaging with something outside of your respective industry. Perhaps you are a litigator who wants to become more engaged with your community by joining the board of a nonprofit. Through this experience, you can gain leadership, management, and programming experience that you can translate over to your legal practice. You will also learn how to navigate board procedure and gain familiarity with governance documents. By being in the decision-maker role, you can better understand how decisions are made when you are working with corporate clients and you can therefore better tailor your legal counsel more effectively. Or, perhaps you enjoy coding on the side. You could create a new app to help streamline team communications within your firm – sort of like Slack but for lawyers.

And second, interdisciplinary thinking can take the form of within industry knowledge – just from a different perspective than your own. For instance, if you are a corporate lawyer, you will passively gain basic working knowledge of various areas like tax, real estate, and employee benefits. If you, for instance, proactively worked to gain additional knowledge in these fields, you would become, *ceteris paribus*, a drastically better legal advisor – especially when game-time decisions are required. At the same time, if you are a tax lawyer who spends time understanding the business of your clients, you can become a more effective tax attorney by ensuring your advice is contextually relevant. Just because a limited liability company is taxed as a corporation doesn't make that company a corporation for business purposes (yes, this is a disagreement that I have actually had in practice). The best tax attorneys that I have worked with are able to translate the relevant tax implications over to the particular corporate transaction because they understood the business operations.

When engaging in interdisciplinary thinking, being able to connect concepts is paramount. If you aren't able to be a connector, then your hard work will not bear fruit. Many of the greatest innovators and entrepreneurs of our time have recognized the important relationship between connectivity and creativity. Studies have shown that the best ideas may come from outside of your immediate industry, so long as there are deep structural analogies between the fields.[26] In one study profiled by the Harvard Business Review, inline skaters, roofers, and carpenters were asked to develop ideas for increasing the comfort and usage of the safety gear that carpenters use. When the ideas were evaluated on the basis of novelty and usefulness, the skaters did the best, then the roofers, and, lastly, the carpenters themselves. The roofers and the skaters shared deep structural analogies with the carpenters in that they all required safety equipment to perform their tasks. This study showed that, so long as there are deep structural analogies, individuals in fields that are further away tend to generate the most novel and useful ideas.[27]

On the other hand, where there aren't deep analogies between two fields, it can be difficult to generate practical and creative ideas. If a group of lawyers and a group of aerospace engineers are tasked with creating a more aerodynamic rocket ship, my money would be on the engineers to come up with better and more creative ideas in almost all cases. There isn't, *prima facie*, a deep enough analogy between both fields for lawyers to be able to ideate more effectively than aerospace engineers about the design of rock ships. At the same time, being able to identify and define exactly what constitutes a structural analogy between one field or another is, in my view, up for creative debate. What may not constitute a structural analogy for one person may constitute a structural analogy for another. In the above example, perhaps one of the lawyers is an intellectual property attorney that was recently conducting diligence on aerodynamic design patents. It's up to the user to be the connector. And the most successful of these go on to become immortalized as innovators.

Fortunately, attorneys tend to be rather academic. So, embarking on a journey of interdisciplinary thinking should be within many attorneys' comfort zones. The hard part is translating that to practice. The key, again, is being able to draw connections.

Let's take a look at how this strategy can be applied in practice. Note that this application section serves as a guide. Depending on your situation, certain steps may or may not be applicable and other steps may be required.

Interdisciplinary Thinking: Organizational Level

Step 1: Identify the task at hand. By accurately defining the task, you can greatly influence your ability to connect your interdisciplinary pursuits down the line.

Let's assume that you define your task as recruiting a more diverse summer class. This initiative is part of a larger push to increase diversity at all levels of your firm.

Step 2: To promote interdisciplinary thinking, consider pulling together a diverse team. See Section 6 to learn more about building interdisciplinary teams. Ask your teammates about their experiences and views on the present task. If you know that a particular teammate worked for a different organization or industry before joining your practice, inquire about any potential insights that could be derived from those experiences.

If your team is already set, consider the possibility of inviting outside colleagues, to the extent appropriate, to share their perspectives and expertise. Outside views, especially from different levels of the organization or from different teams, often spark new insights for discussion and can be a great way to source interdisciplinary knowledge.

To increase the diversity of your summer class, you invite colleagues from across your firm that have shown a commitment to diversity and inclusion. Your colleagues include a junior associate, a mid-level associate, a senior associate, and a partner. Your team reflects a variety of age groups, skill levels, genders, and racial backgrounds.

You encourage your teammates to share their prior experiences, especially because some of your teammates spent time at different firms and others worked in different industries before entering legal practice.

Through these discussions, you learn that one of your teammates worked for a firm ("Firm B") that amended its recruiting efforts to promote greater diversity of its summer class. Rather than follow its prior practice of targeting only a select number of law schools, Firm B added a new school to its list. This school was traditionally underrepresented and the majority of its students were minorities. By including a new law school to its recruiting efforts, Firm B was able to diversify its summer program with broader representation.

Seeing this as a potential opportunity, you ask your teammate to research additional details regarding how Firm B accomplished its task and what the end results were. You also invite another attorney who spent time at Firm B to share her experiences at your next meeting.

Step 3: After exploring your team's existing views, it may be helpful to proactively seek insights from different disciplines. Direct your team members to conduct additional research and regroup at a later meeting.

For the next meeting, you task the rest of your teammates with researching other firms (within your peer group and outside) to see if there are any best practices that your team can learn from. You also ask them to look into other industries that share deep structural analogies (as discussed above) to legal practice, like in finance or consulting, for additional ideas.

Step 4: Consolidate your ideas into an action plan. Present it to any relevant decision makers and incorporate their feedback. A more detailed explanation of getting decision-maker approval can be found in Section 3.2, Questioning the Status Quo: Organizational Level,

Steps 5-8.

Step 5: Act. The more you practice interdisciplinary thinking, the more robust your ideation process will be.

Considerations: Being on the lookout for connections is a helpful practice for interdisciplinary thinking and creativity in general. Inspiration can come from the most unlikely of places and being able to find those points of connectivity can advantage your team.

A major barrier to interdisciplinary thinking is closed-mindedness, which is a psychological limitation that we place upon ourselves. We've all encountered individuals who think their way is the best way on Earth (this can be particularly true in legal practice as attorneys can sometimes feel that they know everything). But when we look at the best practitioners in our respective fields, they are more often than not more open-minded than their less successful peers. When you open your mind, you allow yourself the opportunity to connect the dots between disciplines.

Interdisciplinary Thinking: Individual Level

Step 1: Identify the task at hand. By accurately defining the task, you can greatly influence your ability to connect your interdisciplinary pursuits down the line.

Let's imagine that you recently became a senior attorney. Management, firm citizenship, and business development are now top of mind. How do you effectively manage your new responsibilities while giving yourself the appropriate metrics to benchmark your progress?

Step 2: Look outside the immediate field that your task is categorized in and look for connections. There are two approaches to achieve this. First, you can reflect over your personal experiences. Remember that you are more than just your profession of being an attorney.

Second, you can actively seek new content and experiences. To guide where you look, begin with fields that share deep structural analogies with your present task.

To address the task defined in Step 1, you look towards the business world. You review the best books on management techniques, sales, negotiation, and entrepreneurship. You listen to podcasts and talks from highly effective CEOs and business leaders. And you reconnect with some of your college friends who are now senior consultants. By learning from the business world, you are beginning to gain a better understanding of the mechanics of running a legal practice rather than just learning how to advise on a discrete area of the law.

Step 3: Consolidate your ideas into an action plan and share your ideas with your trusted colleagues. Incorporate any relevant feedback.

After doing your diligence, you have a list of key ideas that you'd like to put into practice, which include: speaking with your firm mentor (yes, even senior attorneys have mentors) to develop appropriate key performance indicators to measure your progress; scheduling business development training with a professional sales coach; and applying collaborative, flat management techniques.

You discuss these ideas with your trusted peers and friends within the firm. You discover that your peers who were also recently promoted are working to address the same challenges. Collectively, your group decides to hold quarterly meetings to discuss best practices and share ideas for growth and development. At your first informal discussion, one of your peers raises the important question of time management, an area that you hadn't yet developed a plan for even though it permeates across all of your action items. Another one of your peers, an ex-banker, suggests using a spreadsheet as a one-stop-shop for tracking your time and workflow. She shares with your group her spreadsheet setup and a few basic best-practices when it comes to operating a program like Microsoft Excel (e.g., pivot tables, vlookup, data validation, conditional formatting, and simple functions).

Step 4: Act. The more you practice interdisciplinary thinking, the more robust your ideation process will be.

After determining that time management is the most important item to address first, as success in managing your schedule will lead to success in the other areas, you build out your spreadsheet and become familiar with Excel. This gives you the push you need to start the other items in your pipeline.

§8
Learn From All Parts Of Your Business

Learn from your team; learn from your customers.

§8.1: Overview

In corporate culture, management and hierarchy reign supreme. Decisions are made at the top and they trickle down to the bottom. If someone from the bottom has an idea, he or she may try to shoot that idea up the food chain…but without a direct channel to management, most ideas are lost in translation. Creating this informational highway is difficult, but it is possible. Bridgewater Associates, the hedge fund founded by Ray Dalio, is a prime example. Employees are encouraged to share dissenting opinions and ideas from all levels of the company. They are even encouraged to give direct feedback to superiors, including the billionaire founder himself. This is so much a part of the company's culture that employees are evaluated on their ability to speak up and express their ideas.[28] This culture promotes creativity in an industry that prizes original thinking. After all, if everyone was making the same investments, no one would make any money. This difference in thinking is what positions Bridgewater as one of the leading hedge funds (if not the best) in the world. In law, original thinking is what separates law firms from being commoditized. If legal analysis was easy, all firms would produce the same results (or artificial intelligence would eliminate the need for lawyers all together). Thus, encouraging our teams to speak up and to listen to one another can also drive value for our firms and clients just as it does for Bridgewater.

Another great example is how Japanese companies like Toyota were able to achieve significant gains in product quality following World War II. Toyota, for instance, was able to develop quality vehicles efficiently by encouraging assembly-line workers to engage with the products. Any worker could halt the assembly line if an issue or problem arose. This instilled a sense of pride in workers and empowered them to work together to produce the best product possible. By assigning this responsibility to all employees, rather than just designated quality control managers, Toyota was able to not only grow into a robust automaker, but it was also able to drive innovation in manufacturing. This tactic, of course, permeates beyond manufacturing – even influencing companies like Pixar.[29] Further, part of the Toyota manufacturing strategy can be reflected in the Japanese term *genchi gembutsu*, which translates into "go and see for yourself."[30] To truly understand your business, you need to get out there and experience the parts of your company for yourself and engage with your team and your customers.

Moreover, companies that learn from all parts of the business can help management development more thoughtful, holistic, and impactful strategies. Similar to the discussions in Sections 6 and 7, this fosters more creative ideation because it promotes diverse and interdisciplinary thinking. By being proactive in engaging employees from throughout the business, employees also begin to feel more valued and more engaged – which has the added benefit of increasing workplace morale. While soliciting feedback and ideas, however, it is important to be authentic in your request. No one likes it when a company superficially asks for employee feedback just because of an outside consultant. It has to be integrated into the culture, which takes time – as all important things do. It is also important for management to listen to feedback from all corners of the business by giving people a voice.

For law firms and legal teams, management has access to such brilliant minds. It's important to tap into this potential, regardless of whether the attorney is junior or whether the individual is part of the staff. From the backend, the administrative staff is also extremely knowledgeable, especially on matters that could make workflow management more efficient. Don't forget to include them in your discussions as well.

In the startup world, incorporating customer feedback is part of the culture. To create the best products, startups must work closely with customers to better understand their preferences and ideas. Armed with this information, startups work to incorporate this feedback to improve their products. Jeff Bezos built Amazon on the premise of being customer obsessed[31] and Steve Jobs personally addressed customer service requests while he was running Apple. [32] In fact, this principle is so engrained in the startup world that the lean startup methodology, one of the most influential startup philosophies of our time, emphasizes the importance of developing minimum viable products to help founders begin the feedback process as quickly as possible.[33]A minimum viable product isn't meant to be perfect or polished nor is it meant to be the prototype; it's meant to be a product that can test how the fundamental business hypothesis of a certain product functions in the market. By launching the minimum viable product, a founder is able to begin the learning process by incorporating customer feedback on how to improve the product.

Although the lean startup methodology is most applicable to tech- and product-based companies, it has many implications for service-based industries like law as well. For example, if you are working to design a new training initiative within your firm, it can help to put together a pilot initiative to test the pros and cons of your project and revise the training initiative based on the feedback you receive. Although attorneys strive for perfection, as a mistake could mean the difference between a guilty or innocent verdict, the threshold for implementing new initiatives is different. A new initiative, a pilot program, or a new operational procedure will not be perfect in the first instance, which means that the faster you can ideate and revise, the faster you can get your idea into full form. This all starts with a minimum viable product (or service or initiative).

§8.2: Application

Law firms and legal teams, on average, are hierarchal. Attorneys, for instance, are designated by their class year at firms: are you a first, third, fifth, seventh, or ninth year associate? And, at least in biglaw, it's a virtual impossibility to skip a year even if you are a rock star. There is also an innate sense of deference offered to partners because law is still one of the few industries that maintain an apprenticeship-type quality. This is not to suggest that whatever a senior attorney says goes. This is just to highlight that there is an acute awareness of seniority in legal practice.

By learning from companies like Bridgewater and the startup world, the legal industry too can reap the benefits of sourcing creativity and innovation from among its ranks. This strategy isn't appropriate for every situation and is typically reserved for more senior attorneys because it requires sourcing feedback from across the organization. For certain initiatives like confidential matters or initiatives that require quick action, this strategy may not be the most effective. For others like creating a new talent pipeline or sourcing best practices, this approach can work well. We can never stop learning, and our colleagues and clients are an invaluable resource as we continue to embrace our curiosities.

Let's take a look at how this strategy can be applied in practice. Note that this application section serves as a guide. Depending on your situation, certain steps may or may not be applicable and other steps may be required.

Learning From All Parts of Your Business: Colleagues

Alternative 1 (Go Around The Table): If you are leading a meeting or a team, simply go around the table and ask for everyone's opinion. Don't ignore the first years or summer associates or even the staff. As Chris Sacca, the billionaire venture capitalist who invested in Twitter,

Uber, and Instagram, notes, "Don't underestimate anyone you come across. Ever. Whether they are a blue-collar worker waiting for the bus or they are the server or bar tender at the restaurant or they are a low-ranking employee. The smartest leaders that I've ever seen have always gone around the room and asked for everybody's opinion."[34] To hit this point home, a surprising number of my former Skadden colleagues and friends were bar tenders and restaurant servers before they went to law school. We never know where people are in their journey, and it's important to respect the potential of people's ideas (unless they give you legitimate reasons not to).

Alternative 2 (Swinging By): Discuss with your existing team members whether it would be appropriate to get feedback from colleagues from different teams or at varying levels. If you prefer an informal approach, try swinging by someone's office for a quick chat or dropping them a line.

Alternative 3 (Meeting Invitation): Discuss with your existing team members whether it would be appropriate to invite colleagues from different teams or colleagues at varying levels to your next meeting to get a balanced perspective. If so, reach out to a few key contacts that you have on these teams and invite them to participate in your next meeting. When inviting others, it's important to exercise your best judgment. If you are a first-year associate, don't call up the managing partner to brainstorm ideas on how to improve your checklist. Do, however, reach out to associates who are senior to you and who you have a good working relationship with. At the same time, if you are a senior partner, it can be helpful to be clear on your ask. A short email saying "Please come to my office" might give someone a heart attack!

Many legal teams have routine meetings like practice group lunches, team lunches, or office breakfasts. These meetings are generally meant to be opportunities for everyone to catch up and socialize outside of work, but these meetings can also be a great time to invite colleagues from other teams or departments to simply share what their teams are working on. This can help build relationships organically and encourage teams to interact and share information to help everyone be more efficient.

Alternative 4 (Special Meeting): Discuss with your existing team members whether it would be appropriate to create a special meeting for gathering input and ideas from other teams. Or, if a meeting isn't required, consider whether shooting out a survey or email to various groups would be helpful. When launching a new candidate assessment tool for interviews, for instance, getting feedback from attorneys at all levels of the organization can be helpful in ensuring that the new tool properly captures what your team is looking for in new hires.

Alternative 5 (Committees): Create a special committee of high performing attorneys from across your organization to shadow executive committees and team leadership. This can help provide leadership with direct access to various parts of the business and this special committee can also help relay important matters from the ground up. This shadow board can also be a great training ground to develop the future leaders of your organization early, which can provide an enormous amount of value (e.g., better skillset and mindset preparation, knowledge continuity, relationship development, etc.).

Considerations: Whether you take an informal or formal approach to learning from your employees and colleagues, taking that first step in considering whether you should invite others into the discussion will empower your team with more knowledge and a more holistic perspective. This strategy isn't meant for every situation and, with practice, you can become effective at pulling together the right people at the right time. In particular, this strategy is great for generating new and creative ideas as well as tackling complex and unusual problems.

If your organization is particularly siloed, this approach can help breakdown those walls and build bridges between your teams. Everyone benefits from more open conversations. Everyone benefits from the free exchange of ideas. And everyone can continue to expand their practice.

Learning From All Parts of Your Business: Clients

Alternative 1 (Breakfast, Lunch, and Dinner): Discuss with your existing team members whether it would be appropriate to solicit feedback and ideas from your clients. You may be testing out a new initiative or would like to get your client's honest feedback on something that happened. This could progress as a conversation over a phone call or, for more detailed matters, over a meal. Clients always enjoy a meal and they also enjoy being part of the process. This can also be a great way to reconnect with clients you haven't worked with in a while or, potentially, new prospects. This process can also signal that your firm is proactively working to improve your business so that you can be an even better legal advisor.

Alternative 2 (Surveys): Discuss with your existing team members whether it would be appropriate to solicit feedback and ideas from your clients. If the initiative you are working on is a larger scale project, your team may wish to contact a large number of clients. It can be helpful to designate a specific team of staff members to help with outreach. A simple and effective way of gathering client feedback is to circulate a simple survey or questionnaire. It could be a form that asks one question (e.g., "let us know how we are doing") with a text field for clients to fill in. Or, it could be a series of questions with ratings (e.g., list on a scale of 1 to 5, with 1 being "Strongly Agree" and 5 being "Strongly Disagree"). In any event, these surveys should take no more than five minutes…or else no one will complete them. I know I sure don't. Collaborating with clients in this manner can be delicate and it can, at times, require clear rules of engagement. For instance, it can be helpful to ensure that: (i) all outreach is consistent and from the same team, and (ii) all responses are monitored and consistent.

Considerations: Getting client feedback can be a particularly sensitive topic and it's important to include the relevant relationship partners or relationship managers. You don't want to upset any clients or your own teammates.

Additionally, legal teams can be particularly sensitive about asking clients for feedback in fear that they will raise issues or problems that reflect negatively on the team or that are systemic in nature. If that's the case, you may actually benefit the most from getting such feedback. By working to address your clients' concerns, you can get ahead of the curve and better differentiate yourself from your peers. Alternatively, if you don't address these concerns, someone else will and that someone will take your client away from you. Be strong enough to have the difficult conversations, because it's only through these conversations that you can strengthen your firm or organization.

Lastly, engaging with your clients and giving them a voice can leave your team with a number of benefits. Often, clients are the parties that are driving change and transformation in the legal sector. Look at what's happening now with diversity and inclusion. Clients are demanding it and legal teams are responding. If you are able to, collaborating with clients on how to improve your team will show that you care and that you are working hard to grow. And that can go a long way.

§9
Ideas-First Culture

Ideas reign supreme.

§9.1: Overview

Ideas over ego. For more creative conversations and solutions, valuing the idea over the person can lead to powerful breakthroughs. Great managers and senior attorneys can be an accelerant for great ideas. But average or bad managers and senior attorneys can be a bottle-neck for creativity and stifle it.

Ray Dalio, the founder of the hedge fund Bridgewater Associates, promotes an ideas-first culture by encouraging everyone in the company to speak their mind and even provide feedback to their superiors, including Dalio himself. In fact, he provides public access to these threads of communication and even shared with the entire company how one of his colleagues, Jim H., openly called him out for being unprepared for a meeting. Dalio calls this radical transparency and idea meritocracy. His company even developed a tool called the Dot Collector to help with determining which ideas are the best to pursue. This tool collects the ideas of meeting participants and then runs them through an algorithm based on factors like rank and merit (based on people's thinking patterns in various fields). Once the Dot Collector is finished processing the inputs, it highlights a variety of outputs to help Dalio and his team develop a plan forward.[35] This ideas-first culture has helped Bridgewater become the largest hedge fund in the world and the fifth most important private company in the country.[36]Although law firms and legal teams will likely not take the Bridgewater approach to radical transparency and idea meritocracy, attorneys can work to adopt these principles at a more comfortable level.

For example, certain firms have eliminated upward-flowing feedback reports because they believe that this feedback is overly biased (i.e., skewed too favorably). This, however, ignores the more difficult question of how those firms can work to generate honest feedback from juniors to seniors. By working to promote a more open and honest work culture where seniors openly solicit criticism, upward-flowing feedback can be more productive and objective. This can help create a more collaborative and effective environment because certain bottlenecks can be identified and addressed (e.g., juniors could recommend that their seniors receive management training to better improve the team workflow). If these potential areas aren't addressed, seniors that are ineffective managers will stay within firms for far too long – driving juniors away and slowing down your team.

How can we approach this? As a senior, invite your juniors to a casual conversation and sincerely ask them for their feedback on how you can be a better manager and attorney. Focus the conversation on you, the senior, and not on the juniors. This shows humility, emotional intelligence, strength, and care. Juniors will appreciate the opportunity to share their thoughts as well, which will help increase team morale. Ideas and criticism should flow both ways to make a more inclusive team.

Ideas, however, aren't just about criticism and feedback. They are about creating something new and better. With firms trying to chart out the future of legal practice, the teams that combine the best ideas with the best execution will lead the pack.

From the senior perspective, hiring the best and the brightest means that you have a team of wonderfully talented attorneys that you can train and empower. Many legal teams focus heavily on the training component but not as much on the empowering one. By encouraging your juniors to share their ideas, you can crowdsource best practices and ideas that can help improve your team and organization. Your team is more than a replaceable body on a deal or case; your team is your most valuable asset. And when we take a step back and look at where innovation comes from, it typically comes from individuals with fresh perspectives (i.e., new entrants) – not the incumbents. Seniority is effective in maintaining the status quo, but juniors can be effective in pushing the needle forward.

From the junior perspective, being bold enough to share your ideas, respectfully, can help differentiate you from your peers and strengthen your team. If you notice an opportunity to contribute, don't be afraid to speak up. Law firms and legal teams can be hierarchal and you have to earn your voice, but good ideas should have legs of their own. Trust in the idea, and be sure to back it up with diligence and a game plan or proposal if appropriate.

Whether you are a senior or junior attorney, being able to provide supporting evidence of your idea is helpful in contextualizing the discussion. For any idea, identifying the following items are key:

1. **Opportunity/Problem.** When identifying the opportunity, be as

clear as possible. Is there an opportunity within your team or organization for capturing more value? Is there an opportunity within the market that your team can capture? Is there something your team can improve to provide more value to clients? Is there a problem that needs to be addressed? If so, what is it...specifically?

2. **Solution.** Identifying the solution should be clear, but it may not be absolutely specific. It's more important to identify the opportunity (or problem) and develop a general direction that the solution could trend towards even if you aren't sure what the precise solution is. For example, you may recognize that your team is being inefficient with fixed-fee matters and that your bottom line is suffering as a result. You may not know what the specific solution is, but you can be clear in charting out a path: pulling together a team to diligence the problem and evaluate possible paths forward. One potential path is to reduce the amount of fixed-fee matters that your team takes on, increase standard fee arrangements, or find areas to scale your efficiency on fixed-fee matters (hint: the solution isn't simply to push work down to the attorneys with the lowest rates). This approach stands contrary to raising the issue and providing no steps forward. This is how you can lose credibility.

3. **Resource requirement.** If possible, it can be helpful (and reduce back and forth conversations) for you to sketch together the potential resources that you need. This may come in the form of human capital, financial backing, marketing support, or something else. This helps communicate to the decision makers what their cost to pursuing this solution is. If the benefits outweigh these costs, your path forward is much more likely to proceed.

4. **Timeline.** Similar to the above, it can be helpful to put together a projected timeline for implementation. For longer-term projects, breaking this timeline into phases can be helpful (e.g., diligence and fact gathering, action items for one year, action items for three years, etc.). This is also where you can identify objective metrics to benchmark your progress (also known as key performance indicators).

5. **Action plan.** This answers the "what's next" question. Determining what immediate steps you can take will significantly improve your odds of getting the commitment you need from your team. Ideally, you can pull together the first four items into a detailed one-page document that you can share with decision makers and team members. The action plan should start with general items and then become more specific over time once you gather more information. Alternatively, diagraming a few key discussion points to start the conversation can also be appropriate.

Walking through these above items will help provide you with some structure to your conversations. Efficiency is key and you want to reduce the amount of back and forth between various parties. You also want to try to pre-empt as many follow-up questions as possible. The worst thing that you can do is be unprepared and waste someone's time.

From another perspective, whenever presenting new ideas, it's our job to convince others that our ideas make sense and should proceed forward. No one else will do that for us.

§9.2: Application

Although attorneys are known to have big egos, the subject matter of legal practice means that there is a silver lining: attorneys prize logic, reason, and rationale above all else. While this, at times, can be difficult to manage – especially for those on the business side – this quality means that attorneys can actually be more open to receiving ideas from throughout the entire team or organization. The ideas just need to be well constructed, researched, and presented. Oh, and, of course, your logic of pursuing your idea must outweigh the logic of maintaining the status quo.

As discussed in Section 8.1, an effective way to propose a new idea is to suggest a pilot. This helps reduce the psychological cost of trying something new because a pilot is a test run meant to pressure test the project or initiative, source feedback, and reduce uncertainty.

Another approach is to appeal to an attorney's innate sense of risk mitigation. By reframing your idea as a means to protect the downside, to reduce risk, and to reduce uncertainty, you can move along the grain rather than against it. For instance, let's imagine that you have an idea to hold a new collaborative workshop with prospects to drive new business. Rather than focusing on the upside of doing something new, which can sometimes be a hard sell to attorneys who find comfort in the status quo, you can make the following point. *By **not engaging** with prospects in new and collaborative ways, you will **lose** new business opportunities to your peers that are. To protect this downside, trying something new like a collaborative workshop with your prospects will **reduce your risk exposure** to competition.*

Achieving an ideas-first culture and work environment requires a team effort, with direction from the top and engagement from across the organization.

Let's take a look at how this strategy can be applied in practice. Note that this application section serves as a guide. Depending on your situation, certain steps may or may not be applicable and other steps may be required.

Alternative 1 (Top Down): If you are a senior attorney on your team or within your organization, you are well positioned to promote an ideas-first culture. Start by encouraging your team members to share their thoughts. Set the stage by checking your ego at the door and invite them to provide you with constructive feedback as well. This really hits the point home. Promoting an open-minded, friendly culture is so important for any work environment but it can be somewhat difficult in legal practice. With the apprenticeship-like culture of legal teams, senior attorneys can feel a sense of entitlement where juniors can feel a sense of overwhelming deference. Ideally, the legal hierarchy should act like a sports team, with a senior attorney acting like a team captain. As a team captain, your role is to promote the success of your team by coordinating and promoting the talent of your team. It's not to suppress it. One of the best senior attorneys that I've worked with told me straight up that his team is flat and encouraged me to share my thoughts and ideas with him – with the caveat that I should do my diligence first. Unsurprisingly, he's regarding as one of the most creative and successful attorneys out there.

Depending on the size of your team, you may wish to start this conversation at a regularly scheduled team meeting or schedule a new one. Start the meeting by laying down the foundation: that you would like to work on promoting a more open culture of ideas. Highlight a few areas that you would like to solicit ideas for (e.g., how to promote a more open culture of ideas, how to improve business development, how to strengthen firm citizenship, etc.) and then propose your initial thoughts on the topic(s). By sharing your ideas first, you can get the conversation flowing by lowering the barrier to entry of being the first person to speak. Then, open up the floor. Encourage your juniors to share their views, even if it stands in contrast to someone more senior. Procedurally, it's important to proceed topic-by-topic rather than throwing out all your ideas for discussion at once. A step-by-step approach will help your team focus their thoughts and flush out all the details. With these details in mind, it can also be easier to draw parallels and best practices between your topics of discussion.

Your first meeting may not result in any specific action items, but you can encourage people to come up with a few ideas for your next meeting. To ride the wave of energy, don't wait a month to regroup. Schedule another touchpoint within the next week. If you let too much time elapse, you'll lose momentum and people will start to get lost in their work. Attorneys are great at executing directives, so this can be a great, comfortable way for you to begin promoting an ideas-first culture with your team or organization.

Over time, you and your team can work to create more organic modes of communicating ideas. Designating time at regularly scheduled meetings is helpful, but also empowering your team to raise ideas as they come up can lead to added benefits. Deformalizing the process, whether through open-door policies or offering coffee breaks, can be powerful. Oh, and an open-door policy only works if it's practiced both ways: juniors won't pop into your office if you don't pop into theirs (this also helps to deformalize the hierarchy). Having worked at two biglaw firms, I can tell you from first-hand experience that the senior attorneys that I had the best relationships with were the ones that made the effort to drop by my office from the very beginning. The seniors that I never brainstormed with were the ones that never swung by – even if we sat on the same floor. And yes, there was a positive correlation with the success rates of the senior attorneys that swung by my office and didn't.

Alternative 2 (Bottom Up): If you are a junior attorney, engaging with other attorneys and sharing your ideas will help promote an ideas-first culture. Cultural changes will need buy-in from the top, but, if you are able to make your voices heard, the top will listen. Consider the principle of strength in numbers. If you have an idea to improve the process of entering time, it can help to have this discussion with your peers and test out your idea. Let's imagine that your organization is looking to improve the timeliness of time entries. Some attorneys may take down their time every day and then enter that into the time-keeping program. Others might take down their time every day but only enter their time at the end of the week. And, still, others might take down their time whenever they can and hand their time sheets to their secretaries to enter in at the end of the month, creating a traffic jam in workflow for secretaries every four weeks. This leads to challenges in monitoring workflow, inaccuracies in billable time, and late time entries that can cause clients headaches. Your solution may be to designate automatically generated reminders to attorneys who let an entire week go by without an entry. After three reminders, attorneys must meet with their team leaders and a portion of their bonus may be deducted after a certain number of strikes. Proposing an idea of this magnitude will require some diligence and support, and going through the process of identifying the problem, the solution, the resource requirements, the timeline, and the action plan is key when presenting it to your seniors. By speaking with your peers, and potentially running a simulation of how this can incentivize timely reporting (or disincentivize untimely reporting), you can highlight that you did your homework. Additionally, having peers support this initiative provides your seniors with a sense of validation (e.g., 90% of your peers are in favor), which can potentially be enough to convince your seniors to give you the green light to move forward, which may include a larger scale test or straight implementation. If this idea sounds crazy to you, this is a strategy that is actually employed by some of the most successful law firms in the world.

Another consideration is to leverage your relationships with senior attorneys. If you have a good relationship with a partner, for instance, you may have the ability to share your thoughts casually during a phone call, coffee, or by dropping by her office. Alternatively, if you don't have that relationship, perhaps one of your peers does. Or, you may need to develop that relationship. Remember to always be respectful, because a junior attorney proposing certain ideas to seniors can come off the wrong way. Emotional intelligence is important to keep in mind when embracing creative thinking.

Many teams also have mentorship programs. Leveraging these programs can also be an organic way to raise ideas as your mentor can help make introductions and open doors for you.

Considerations: As you and your team begin to promote an ideas-first practice, your ability to distinguish between value-generating ideas and non-value-generating ideas will sharpen. Like with any skill, it takes time to learn how to evaluate which ideas to pursue and which ideas not to pursue.

There will also be times where all the data may point towards pursuing one idea over the other, but, as timing or external factors would have it, that idea didn't work out. And that is okay. I repeat. That is okay. This process isn't about generating a 100% success rate. It's about going through the process to determine the best possible outcome. Sometimes it means going down the wrong path to find the right one. And sometimes that wrong path may become the right path in due course.

There's also an inherently fun component to putting ideas first. When this happens, we can all encounter fresh perspectives that can energize and refresh us. We can learn something new. And we exercise a different part of our minds.

§10
Design Thinking

A humancentric approach to serving your clients.

§10.1: Overview

Design thinking is a humancentric problem-solving strategy based on the intersectionality of three factors[37]:

1. **Desirability**. Is something desirable from the human perspective?
2. **Viability**. Is something viable from the economic perspective?
3. **Feasibility**. Is something feasible from the technological perspective?

With these three guiding factors in mind, the process of undergoing design thinking consists of five phases[38]:

1. **Frame a question**. What is the driving question that requires solving? Are you asking the right questions?
2. **Gather inspiration**. What do people actually need? Work with and observe your clients and your team.
3. **Generate ideas**. Ideate past the immediate and obvious ideas.
4. **Make ideas tangible**. Prototype.
5. **Test to learn**. Get feedback from your team and clients.
6. **Share the story**. Inspire others with your story.

Going through these five phases in the context of desirability, viability, and feasibility can help you and your team better understand the needs of your organization and your clients, develop more innovative initiatives to address these needs, and implement such initiatives more efficiently while mitigating risks.

Popularized by the renowned design firm, IDEO, design thinking has greatly influenced startup practices in the past few decades. More recently, established companies have been turning to firms like IDEO to bring a designer's perspective to their business challenges. Relatedly, companies have also been espousing design thinking internally by encouraging its practice in teams across the organization.[39]

Design thinking, as a process, has had many successes over the years. Apple hired IDEO in 1980 to design the first usable mouse for the Lisa computer when previous attempts were too expensive (viability) and challenging to produce (feasibility). By going through the design thinking process, IDEO was able to successfully develop the first usable mouse, a design which permeates through most computer mice to date. In the world of computers, IDEO was also able to help translate bulky computers into the first notebook-style devices for GRiD systems in the 1980s.[40]

But design thinking isn't just for tech. IDEO has applied this practice to help Fender design new acoustic amps, Julep design better nail polish wands, IKEA design the future kitchen, Lee Jeans develop a jade-infused cooling denim, Levi's develop its touch-enabled Commuter Trucker Jacket, and various medical companies better manage treatments.[41] And companies like Nordstrom, Bank of America, Starbucks, and GE Healthcare have also adopted design thinking internally to launch new products, apps, and initiatives.[42]

To materialize this concept, let's walk through how IDEO was able to apply design thinking to help Oral B. Oral B hired IDEO to help it design a better children's toothbrush. Conventional wisdom suggested that a children's toothbrush should be like an adult's…just smaller and shorter to fit a child's hands. But when IDEO took the time to fact gather in the field by observing how children were *actually* brushing their teeth, it made a discovery: children hold their toothbrushes differently than adults. Adults tend to hold toothbrushes with their fingers whereas children hold them in in their palms. This difference in dexterity meant that the smaller and shorter children's toothbrushes that were the market standard were promoting kids to damage their gums because of how they were holding the toothbrushes. To fix this problem, IDEO helped Oral B design a wider toothbrush to fit within children's palms. By deviating from the market standard (at the time) and going into the field, rather than relying on assumption, IDEO was able to help Oral B design the leading children's toothbrush for 18 consecutive months before the market conformed.[43] This is the power of design thinking. Learn and observe from your market by getting your hands dirty like a designer.

§10.2: Application

Design thinking can be applied to legal practice in a number of ways. Academic initiatives like the Stanford Legal Design Lab[44] and the Penn Law Future of the Profession Initiative[45] are teaching classes on how design thinking can be applied to improve legal services. The Stanford Legal Design Lab, for instance, focuses on developing new initiatives to help promote equity and access to the civil justice system and researching how new technology and policies can drive innovation in law.

As design thinking is itself a creative problem-solving strategy, legal teams that wish to employ this approach can follow the six steps mentioned above. They can also incorporate creative problem-solving approaches mentioned in this playbook into the various design thinking stages. Designers seek inspiration from a myriad of sources and design thinking is inclusive rather than exclusive.

Let's take a look at how this strategy can be applied in practice. Note that this application section serves as a guide. Depending on your situation, certain steps may or may not be applicable and other steps may be required.

Step 1: Pull together a diverse team that is committed to studying the design thinking approach (see Section 6 for a discussion on building diverse teams). Design thinking has a rich history and legal teams can diligence many case studies just as they would case law.

Step 2: Run through the design thinking steps.

1. Frame a question. *How do we improve work-life balance and happiness?*
2. Gather inspiration. *Study how the world's most efficient business people manage their time and workload. Study how the world's most profitable businesses, particularly in finance and consulting due to the underlying structural similarities, work to improve their employees' work-life balance. Study how technology companies are working to make their employees happier.*
3. Generate ideas. *Refer to the strategies in this playbook to assist with idea generation. For instance, see Section 5 (Generate More Ideas), Section 7 (Embrace Interdisciplinary Thinking), and Section 12 (Think Like An Entrepreneur). Refer to other strategies of ideation. Google search. Talk to friends and colleagues. Will ping pong tables and free food make attorneys happier? Will designating certain firm citizenship work as billable help? Will decreased facetime requirements*

and increased work location flexibility help?

4. Make ideas tangible. *Choose an idea or two to prototype.*
5. Test to learn. *Get feedback from your attorneys. What did they like? What didn't they like? Involve them in the ideation process.*
6. Share the story. *After implementing the initiative, create a case study, write an article, or create a video to share with the market.*

Considerations: Empower that team with the ability to connect with other members of your organization, clients, or others, as applicable. Design thinking is a humancentric approach that requires involving the key stakeholders, whether through direct involvement during ideation or through observation. This is also especially important for the testing and prototyping phase as feedback must be incorporated to revise and strengthen the underlying service or product.

Give your team the flexibility to go against the grain by challenging established assumptions (see Section 3 for a discussion on challenging the status quo).

Don't be afraid to try something new and ultimately fail. Going through the design thinking steps will help you minimize risk by going through an established process; however, there is still some degree of risk present with any new initiative. If an attempt fails, don't immediately disband the team. A failure may inform the next success and a failure does not mean a failure of the team or the design thinking process/initiative; it could highlight a bigger challenge that needs to be addressed.

§11
Low Investment, High Impact

A creativity filter for identifying effective, practical initiatives.

§11.1: Overview

The majority of this playbook focuses on ways that you and your team can generate new and creative ideas. This section focuses on a powerful strategy for evaluating which ideas to pursue in a legal setting: the low-investment, high-impact approach to idea selection. This strategy has two parts. First, which ideas can be implemented with low investment? Second, of these ideas, which ones can leave the greatest impact on your team or organization?

Low-investment ideas are those that require little investment in money and human capital. High-impact initiatives are those that, when implemented, create a material, marginal benefit for the legal team and organization. Would the idea improve your team's effectiveness or efficiency? Would the idea make your team happier? Would the idea help strengthen your team's culture? If the answer to these questions or ones like these are "maybe" or "sort of" – then the ideas in question are not high impact and should be discarded.

Because legal teams tend to be more conservative when implementing new initiatives, this low-investment, high-impact approach fits nicely within the natural risk tolerance of attorneys. It reduces the psychological and financial burden of pursuing initiatives in areas that attorneys aren't traditionally trained in like business development, firm citizenship, process management, and organizational behavior. It also increases the odds of success because low-investment, high-impact approaches tend to be the ones that are smaller in scale and less complex (i.e., less things can go wrong). They are the low-hanging fruit, which often can mean that these ideas should have already been put into place or that these ideas can be implemented with relative ease.

From a timing perspective, low-investment, high-impact approaches typically favor shorter-term initiatives because short-term projects generally require lower investments. This means that a new idea can be implemented successfully in a short amount of time to quickly benefit your team and organization or it can fail fast so that another idea can be pursued.

An added benefit of applying this strategy in legal practice is that it can help build your team's fluency with developing new initiatives in a low-cost environment. Especially in the beginning, this can help your team develop greater confidence and skill in creative problem solving and can be a great pathway towards tackling larger, more complex ideas.

§11.2: Application

In corporate law, there is a concept known as the "business judgment rule," which generally provides deference to the decisions of corporate boards if such boards made such decisions with due care and in good faith – even if the decisions were suboptimal. When working on implementing a new initiative for your team or organization, due care and good faith should also be the cornerstones of deciding which ideas to pursue. By having thoughtful conversations and debates, analyzing your options, and ensuring different perspectives are considered, you can help ensure that your decision-making process is sound – even if the resulting initiative fails.

The low-investment, high-impact approach can be a helpful tool for your team when evaluating the appropriate course of action. By discussing which ideas can make it through this filter, you are taking the steps to ensure that you are making decisions with due care and in good faith. This approach is one of many idea filters that you can use and should not be interpreted as the only defining threshold for your discussions.

Let's take a look at how this strategy can be applied in practice. Note that this application section serves as a guide. Depending on your situation, certain steps may or may not be applicable and other steps may be required.

> **Alternative 1 (Filter):** After your team has developed a set of ideas, apply the low-investment, high-impact approach to isolate those initiatives that require low financial or human capital investments but yield high impacts to your team.

In evaluating the required investment, create objective and consistent measures that you can use to compare and contrast your ideas. From a financial perspective, will the initiative require $1,000, $10,000, or $100,000? Depending on the size of your balance sheet, some or all of these may be considered low investment (or high investment). From an organizational standpoint, do you have enough people power to implement the initiative? Can the initiative be completed with your initial ideation team or does it need to be expanded? Will this project be led by attorneys, staff, or a combination of the two? Will pursuing this project lead to an undue time burden on attorneys (the billable hour still reigns supreme)?

In evaluating the degree of impact, will the implemented initiative provide a material, marginal benefit to your team and organization? How many people will your initiative benefit? Will your initiative lead to short-term benefits or long-term ones? Will your team and organization be better off with the idea implemented? Should this idea already have been implemented?

Alternative 2 (Ideation): The low-investment, high-impact approach is an effective filter, but it can also serve as a useful ideation tool. This can be especially helpful for non-profits or legal teams with smaller budgets. What can you do for free that requires little planning and people power but still provides material benefits? What resources can you leverage? Can you automate anything? Are there prior programs that you put on that you can repurpose? Or, are there members of your team that have experience implementing initiatives in another setting that they can apply to yours? To get the juices flowing, it can be helpful to ask your team what initiatives they've worked on recently or within the past year.

§12
Think Like An Entrepreneur

Relentless improvement – for your clients and your business.

§12.1: Overview

Walk into any Fortune 100 company and chances are that you will encounter the concept of *entrepreneurial thinking*. Walk into any Am Law 100 firm and you'll hear crickets. As the legal industry is reactive, it is one of the last industries to not embrace the power of entrepreneurial thinking. Smaller firms and in-house teams are in many ways required to think entrepreneurially to survive in the market or to function as part of the corporate body. Larger firms, however, tend to struggle with this concept because attorneys are not predisposed to be entrepreneurial on their own accounts. Lawyers are meant to mitigate risk, not thrive on it. In many ways, the prototypical attorney is antithetical to the prototypical entrepreneur – and they can drive each other crazy when they work together. Entrepreneurs operate through trial by fire whereas attorneys need an order of operations. Entrepreneurs will build the boat while they are headfirst into the water. Attorneys will read the instruction manual twice over before picking up a hammer. Society needs both and there is nothing wrong with either approach, but each group has something to learn from the other. Where entrepreneurs can learn to ensure that corporate formalities are checked when starting new ventures and papering key agreements, attorneys can learn to think creatively and focus on solving problems and improving systems.

First things first: entrepreneurs are not reckless. Entrepreneurs are calculated and strategic. They conduct detailed market analyses, business plans, financial projections, and strategies to protect the downside. They do, however, act on opportunities they uncover, similar to how investors search for undervalued companies. Entrepreneurs take the risk of action because their motivation to change the world outweighs their fear of failure. Fundamentally, entrepreneurs act on their ideas and take accountability.

Strategically, entrepreneurs listen to their customers, find new and creative ways to better solve and address customer needs and wants, and practice a bit of business jiu jitsu. To be successful, they have to constantly be learning. It's not enough to be an industry expert – entrepreneurs are working to expand a field and thus need to learn and create knowledge at the same time. If, for instance, an entrepreneur is working to develop a new form of Wi-Fi, she needs to be an industry expert (or become an industry expert) in existing Wi-Fi technologies as well as experiment to push that field forward. There's no guidebook to the next iteration of something, we have to create it.

Fundamental to any entrepreneur is the ability to operate a business. It doesn't matter how great your product or service is if you can't generate positive cashflow. To do this, entrepreneurs need to build successful teams with diverse talents. They need to empower their teams and listen to their ideas because you can only change the world with a team behind you.

Distilled, thinking like an entrepreneur includes, among other things, embracing ambiguity, looking for opportunities of improvement, being creative, solving problems, and seeing the bigger picture.

§12.2: Application

Applying entrepreneurial thinking to legal practice is not as big of a hurdle as it may seem on its face. While entrepreneurs and attorneys do tend to exhibit antithetical traits, they also have many parallel and overlapping qualities: dedication to clients, work ethic, the ability to provide clarity to complexity, and the ability to develop solutions for clients. Attorneys are, by definition and in accordance with the applicable rules of ethics, required to advocate on behalf of their clients to the fullest of extent of their abilities. This includes burning the midnight oil for their clients and helping their clients navigate the complex web of regulations, statutes, case law, and precedent. The overarching goal of any attorney is to help create solutions for their clients, regardless of the outlook. Attorneys will take a position and defend it until the end, just like an entrepreneur with a brilliant idea.

The foundation is already there for attorneys to think like entrepreneurs. They already act entrepreneurially for their clients and they aren't afraid to take on the odds in practice. Thus, by refocusing this skill towards themselves, attorneys can tap into their entrepreneurial mindset, think forward, and focus on improving themselves and their teams.

Let's take a look at how this strategy can be applied in practice. Note that this application section serves as a guide. Depending on your situation, certain steps may or may not be applicable and other steps may be required.

Alternative 1 (Become The Client): Pretend that you are your own client. Think about what challenges you are looking to overcome or what practices you wish to streamline or improve. Rather than positioning them as your own initiatives, take a step back and abstract away. Pretend that you are approaching these challenges and opportunities on behalf of a third party.

If my client came to me with these questions, how and what would I advise?

By becoming the client, you can get into a mindset that you are already familiar with. You can tap into that entrepreneurial drive that you have for your clients and redirect that same energy towards yourself. The key point to remember is to act. Attorneys are comfortable with laying out potential pathways for clients. They create optionality but they rarely have to be the decision maker. Here, you'll need to conduct your own analysis of which pathway makes the most sense for you and act. Once you make this decision, pursue it to its logical end just like with any other client.

Alternative 2 (The "Entrepreneurial Person"): We were all introduced to our imaginary best friend in law school: the reasonable person. From the "reasonable person standard" in criminal law and torts, we were trained to think about what a "reasonable person" would do in a given circumstance. Applying this same intellectual and empathetic exercise to creative thinking, we can make a new friend: the *"Entrepreneurial Person."* Rather than asking yourself what you would do in a given situation, you can ask what an entrepreneur would do. Perhaps you are looking for new ways to engage clients virtually or are looking to drive efficiency for fixed-fee arrangements. What would an entrepreneur do to resolve these scenarios? What would Jeff Bezos, Elon Musk, Peter Thiel, Sarah Blakely, Oprah Winfrey, Bill Gates, Reed Hastings, Daymond John, or Barbara Corcoran do? To imagine what these greats would do, it can be helpful to read their writings, watch their interviews, and follow their stories. This can help you better get into their minds.

If you choose to start following some or all of the above entrepreneurs, you may notice a common thread: hard work is a must. But their definition of hard work is very different from an attorney's. Hard work isn't just about billing as many hours as possible. Hard work is about outworking your competition efficiently. How can you scale your time? How can you automate your work? How can you produce the same quality and amount of work as ten versions of yourself? Working hard can get you up the mountain, but working smart can take you to the skies. This is especially important for attorneys that rely on the billable hour as a metric for performance to keep in mind.

You can also use this method to be proactive as well. Instead of waiting for a situation to arise, you can shift your focus to the business of your practice and ask what the Entrepreneurial Person would do. An entrepreneur may pick up the phone, talk to clients, and get their feedback to help isolate potential areas of improvement. Or, an entrepreneur may take some time to think about how his or her teams are functioning. Entrepreneurs are forward looking and they think about their business holistically – they want to know what they can improve and do better. They don't fall prey to repetition or the status quo, because that means death in the startup world. In legal practice, repetition and the status quo are the market standard. Just imagine what you can do by breaking that trend. And if you can't imagine it, ask your new best friend the Entrepreneurial Person.

Alternative 3 (Business Tools): Don't be afraid to learn and make use of business tools like the SWOT analysis discussed in Section 4, Porter's Five Forces, the Innovation Curve, the Lean Startup methodology, the Good to Great strategy, and more.

SWOT: Take some time to think about your team's strengths, weaknesses, opportunities, and threats. Discuss these items with your team and see how you can make your team and your services better. Turn the scope inwards and apply the SWOT analysis to yourself as well.

Porter's Five Forces: Take some time to think about your competition, the potential for new entrants, the power of your suppliers, the power of your customers, and the threat of substitutes. For law firms, the threat of substitutes (e.g., another law firm) is high – even if you are in the upper echelon.[46]

The Innovation Curve (also known as the Diffusion of Innovation Theory): Understanding how innovations are adopted by the market can help you and your team plan for rolling out new and innovative solutions. The curve is a standard bell curve, flowing from the

"Innovators" to the "Early Adopters" to the "Early Majority" to the "Late Majority" and finally to the "Laggards."[47] Understanding which groups you need to target first, how they respond to imperfect products or services, whether they are the best group to provide you with feedback on new services or products, and how to jump from one segment of the curve to another can help demystify the practice of being creative and testing out new initiatives.

The Lean Startup: Typically applied to tech startups, this approach focuses on how you can build minimum viable products to test out a new initiative before going all in. It also teaches you to be agile and reduce wasteful or unproductive behavior.[48]

Good to Great: The defining principle here is the concept that great businesses are like flywheels – they build momentum. To push the flywheel forward, consideration must be given to: (i) "Level 5" leaders who are focused on the advancement of the business and not themselves; (ii) the who before the what (getting the right people on the bus before figuring out where to go); (iii) the brutal facts while still maintaining hope; (iv) the hedgehog concept of finding your passion, finding what you're best at, and determining what makes you money; (v) creating a culture of discipline; and (vi) searching for technology accelerators (like artificial intelligence, software to manage documents, phone apps, etc.). These six considerations are additive and they compound on each other to drive the wheel forward.[49]

§13
Act

Success is action.

§13.1: Overview

Creativity is an imprecise task that requires getting your hands dirty, experimenting, and trying things that may stretch you beyond your comfort zone. At first, creative thinking and creative problem solving can seem like a monumental task, especially for attorneys focused on bringing analytical structure to the amorphous nature of the law. But, by taking a moment to let the creativity vibes settle in, we can see the parallel that creativity seeks to bring structure to complexity. Solving complex problems in a rapidly evolving world requires creative problem solving – if the solution existed, then the problem wouldn't be complex.

In this section, I bring in insights from a number of entrepreneurs because they represent the epitome of action – they act against the consensus to bring out ideas, services, products, and companies that challenge the status quo, solve problems, make our lives easier, entertain us, and are simply fun to engage with. In law school, we learned to get into the minds of the judges who were interpreting the law. In practice, we learned to get into the mindset of the best practitioners. And, for our creative endeavors, we must take a page out of the gold standard of action: entrepreneurs. Recall our new best friend the Entrepreneurial Person from Section 12.

Whether you choose to implement the creative strategies discussed in this playbook or others, the key to developing successful solutions and implementing new initiatives is to act. Ideas hold no value if they aren't executed. As Jack Dorsey, the founder of Twitter, notes: "The hardest thing to do is start. You have all these ideas. Everyone has an idea. It's really about executing the idea and building the idea and attracting people to help you work on the idea. But the way to begin is to get the idea out of your head, draw it out, talk about it, program it if you are a programmer, or make it if you are building something...."[50]

As attorneys, we can overthink and overanalyze the situation, but we can't let this paralyze us from taking that crucial step forward. A brilliant idea is worthless if its left in the ether. We have to materialize it. And just like any big case or deal, the creative process is rarely linear. We need to have the right team and the right mindset to manage the pivots and charge forward.

Throughout this process, don't be afraid of failure and don't be afraid of making mistakes. Mistakes will happen. It's a learning process. Creativity requires us to learn from these failures so that we can develop a product or service that is better than before. Eric Ries, the brilliant mind behind the lean startup methodology, notes that one of the most important aspects of applying the scientific method to building a company is understanding experimentation: if you cannot fail, you cannot learn.[51] As Mark Zuckerberg, the founder of Facebook, says, "You are going to make tons of mistakes. The important thing is actually learning quickly from your mistakes and not give up."[52] Ray Dalio, the founder of Bridgewater Associates, believes that we should "create a culture in which it is okay to make mistakes and unacceptable not to learn from them."[53] He also notes that, "intelligent people who embrace their mistakes and weaknesses substantially outperform their peers who have the same abilities but bigger ego barriers."[54] (This is especially true for attorneys.) From a different perspective, Sara Blakely, the billionaire founder of Spanx, notes how her father encouraged her to fail...because if she wasn't failing she wasn't trying.[55] Failure, as we can see, is an integral part to success. Its existence is as certain as any other natural law like gravity. And when this happens, you have a decision. Do you let your failures infect your mind and ambition or do you let your failures fuel your successes? As Rocky Balboa famously said: "It's about how hard you can get hit and keep moving forward. How much you can take and keep moving forward. That's how winning is done!"[56]

Action is about forward progress over time. Stay dedicated to the creative process because the legal profession can only progress if we move it forward. The most important thing that you can do to apply creative thinking to your practice is to start and act.

§13.2: Application

There is a principle in psychology known as self-efficacy, a principle uncovered by the Stanford psychologist Albert Bandura, which the American Psychological Association defines as "an individual's belief in his or her capacity to execute behaviors necessary to produce specific performance attainments....Self-efficacy reflects confidence in the ability to exert control over one's own motivation, behavior, and social environment."[57]   Psychologist Angela Duckworth, a professor of psychology at the University of Pennsylvania and the author of *Grit: The Power of Passion and Perseverance*, summarizes the implications of self-efficacy beautifully: if you try to accomplish hard things over and over again and you finally succeed, you begin to build confidence and believe in your capabilities.[58] These principles highlight how working hard to overcome challenges to achieve your goals can help you strengthen your confidence. In applying creative problem solving to legal practice, you and your team will start to build confidence in your abilities as you progress over time. Rather than tackling a large, systemic problem at the outset, consider taking on smaller challenges to build your confidence and find your team's flow (e.g., the low-investment, high-impact initiatives discussed in Section 11). Creative problem solving is very much like breaking in new shoes – there will be sores in the beginning, but the more you wear them, the more comfortable they will become until they are perfectly form fitted.

To help break in your creative problem-solving shoes, there are a few best-practices that can be implemented to drive action on your ideas.

- **Create the right team.** The most valuable asset of any company is its people. The same is true of any team. Especially when you are working to solve a complex problem or create a new initiative, your team can determine whether or not you succeed. In a legal setting, finding the right balance of attorneys and staff is crucial. Depending on the situation, the attorneys may take point with a team of supporting staff or the staff may take point with a team of supporting attorneys. It's also important to create a team with varied skills and from various levels of the organization if possible. And because attorneys bill by the hour, finding attorneys that actually have the capacity to contribute and commit to your initiatives is crucial. Without people, an idea won't move forward. We've all been part of initiatives that have fizzled out because someone somewhere dropped the ball. This, at times, can't be helped because it can be hard to anticipate future workflow in practice. But, there tends to be certain individuals who have a better ability to manage their time than others. Find these people and get them on your team. Find the self-starters and balance your team with ideas-oriented individuals, execution-specialists, and support members. Following the theme of diversity in creativity, pulling together individuals with varied skillsets, backgrounds, and experiences can help improve your team's ability to ideate and execute initiatives (see Section 6 for a discussion on diverse teams). By applying creative problem solving to your practice, you can promote efficiency for your team, create additional value for your clients, and drive business development opportunities for your organization.

- **Establish the right mindset.** From the business perspective, attorneys can sometimes fall into the trap of being lawyers first and problem solvers second. With creative problem solving (and addressing the business of legal practice), the order of operations needs to be flipped. To establish the right mindset, setting the tone at your first team meeting is critical. By flattening the hierarchy, promoting collaboration, driving inclusivity, and opening yourself and your team up for experimentation, you can steer your team through enhanced problem solving. To solve those sticky problems and develop new and improved initiatives, team members need to be primed that there is no clear path forward – one must be made. To paraphrase Ben Horowitz: there are no silver bullets for this – just a lot of lead bullets.[59] The parallel in legal practice is developing a novel argument because no case law or statute provides clarity to your given situation. You pull your team together, construct the best arguments that you can make by drawing upon your resources, and you push forward to defend your client fervently regardless of the odds. Creative problem solving requires a similar resolve, and adopting the right mindset can make or break your team. One helpful approach is to think like a founder and embrace uncertainty as opportunity (see Section 12 for a discussion on thinking like an entrepreneur).
- **Loop in decision makers.** At the earliest reasonable point, it can help to loop in the appropriate decision makers. They can help you further vet your ideas and provide you with the necessary approvals and resources. Before pitching your ideas to the decision makers, however, be sure to spend enough time thinking through your idea. You don't need to present something perfect, but you do need to present something thoughtful.
- **Create an action plan.** Attorneys are particularly adept at understanding and developing processes. Whether tasked with tactfully navigating various court procedures and deadlines or laying down the steps towards signing and closing a deal, attorneys provide value by bringing clarity in these spaces for clients. Here, attorneys must develop a procedural action plan

for implementing their ideas. There are many ways that these action plans can be structured, but consider the following items to help guide your roadmap (in checklist format of course!):

- ☐ Identify the specific opportunity.
- ☐ Define the discrete solution or idea.
- ☐ Conduct your diligence and research.
- ☐ Estimate the costs and resources required (e.g., additional team members, specialized expertise like in tech or marketing, funding).
- ☐ Identify key decision makers that you need buy-in from.
- ☐ Develop an implementation timeline (and break this up into phases if applicable).
- ☐ Determine what your key performance metrics are to measure your progress (e.g., billable hours saved (for efficiency driven initiatives); number of attorneys reached (for firm citizenship initiatives); and growth in reference (for business development initiatives)).

To close out this discussion on action, I would be remiss to leave out one of the most powerful quotes of all time. As Master Yoda proclaimed, "Do or do not. There is no try."[60]

PART III: Creativity in Law

§14
Creative Perspectives

A few additional thoughts.

§14.1: Other Strategies

In Part II, we discussed eleven creative problem-solving strategies that are apt for legal practice. The beauty of creativity, however, is that there isn't an upper limit to the number of strategies that we use. We can always learn more, adapt more, and create more.

For example, if you are looking to deepen your understanding of the law, you may wish to look into how certain entrepreneurs and Nobel Prize winners approach their subject matter. Elon Musk, for instance, reasons with "first principles" rather than defaulting to analogy.[61] This requires breaking down the building blocks of some concept to its core and then building it back up. This technique is also a fundamental tenet to logical reasoning and was employed by Rene Descartes in his famous "I think, therefore I am" piece in his Discourse on Method.[62] Alternatively, you may look into Dr. Richard Feynman, a Nobel Prize-winning physicist. The Feynman technique is one that promotes deep learning by ensuring that you can distill complex ideas into simple terms. This technique consists of three steps: (i) pick a topic to research, (ii) explain the topic to a child using only simple terms (or pretend that you are explaining the topic to a child), and (iii) isolate and review those areas that you find difficult to explain or simplify.[63]

You may also discover powerful strategies by accident. Perhaps you were watching *Sherlock*, the BBC series starring Benedict Cumberbatch as Sherlock Holmes, and stumbled upon a strategy that Sherlock uses known as the mind palace[64] – a memory technique that uses spatial visualization to enhance recall.[65] To improve your memory of certain statutes, e.g., from the tax code, you may wish to adopt this technique to mentally store long lists of information about corporate exemptions.

Lastly, you may wish to create your own strategies. When existing solutions or approaches don't work (either because they aren't applicable or because they weren't effective), you may have to create your own. There isn't a right or wrong way of approaching this task, except that the only way to determine whether or not a particular approach works is to experiment and test it out. Your new creative strategy may be to apply your musical background to form teams as you would an orchestra or quartet – with a focus towards promoting harmony and balance. Or, your new strategy may be to capitalize on new and emerging economies. I don't mean emerging markets like those of developing nations or emerging companies like startups (though there can be correlations). I mean new types of economies altogether. Take the 2008 financial crisis as an example. This period gave birth to the sharing economy, a new economy defined by the shared use of common services and goods, and companies like Airbnb, Uber, and Lyft skyrocketed. Before this time, renting out your bedroom or driving other people around in your personal vehicle for money seemed like an insane idea. But people needed to find ways to bring in extra cash (or save more money) and these types of practices became very real opportunities. Firms that were able to work with these types of companies as they rode the wave of a new economic class were able to develop highly profitable relationships. Extrapolating from this, you may be interested in evaluating new potential clients in 2021, as a global health pandemic is reshaping business views on the future of work. Finding companies that are able to excel once we emerge from our quarantines will be key to developing your next pipeline of clients. Although the term "virtual economy" is already taken (referencing digital economies that exist in video games), the concept may take on new meaning over the next few years…or perhaps crypto is key.

§14.2: Defining The Problem/Opportunity

Creative problem solving starts with the problem or opportunity. Developing an intentional definition, whether general or precise, will have a major impact on the types of ideas your team comes up with. If you define your problem or opportunity incorrectly, this will lead to focusing your team towards the wrong ends and wasting time and resources. Getting this correct the first time or being able to revise your definition upon the discovery of new information can exponentially improve your odds of success.

For example, let's imagine that two managing partners at two different firms are facing the same situation: a declining financial position over the past two years. Partner A from Firm A defines the problem/opportunity as:

"develop a strategy to increase *profits*." Partner B from Firm B defines the problem/opportunity as "develop a strategy to increase *revenue*." Under Partner A's definition, a strategy to decrease expenses would fall within those parameters because profit = revenue – expenses. By decreasing expenses (e.g., eliminating summer lunches and dinners – just kidding!), firm profits would increase. That strategy, however, would not work under Partner B's definition, who asked for an increase in revenue. Definitionally, increasing revenue requires an increase in cashflow (e.g., increasing the number of matters the firm receives from existing clients, increasing the number of firm clients, increasing billable hour rates, or increasing the number of revenue generators (knowledge management, thought leadership, marketing)). As attorneys readily know, the difference that one word can make is astronomical.

To assist with defining the problem or opportunity, you may choose to rely on some of the strategies we discussed in Part II like questioning the status quo (Section 3), identifying pressure points (Section 4), embracing interdisciplinary thinking (Section 7), and/or learning from all parts of your business (Section 8).

§14.3: Focus Forward.

Creativity is about building forward momentum through all of the twists and turns that inevitably arise. By focusing forward, something magical happens in our minds. We become more determined and we become more resilient. In this way, creative problem solving is a bit like running a marathon. When you start the race, you have a literal finish line ahead of you. If it starts to storm, you will grind your way through the race with wet, heavy clothes and soggy, spongy shoes. Nothing is going to stop you from finishing that race. If, however, you were planning on a joy run and it started to storm, you'd be significantly less motivated to finish your run. The difference in these two scenarios is that the marathon focuses you towards completing the 26.2 miles whereas a joy run is open ended. Creativity is the same way. By focusing on your end goal, you put yourself into a problem-solving mindset. You'll innovate through or work around any obstacles that come up to reach your goal.

Focusing on your end goal also puts you into the perspective of "how can we get to point B?" instead of "where can we go from point A?". This minor distinction is important because of how it frames our responses. In the latter scenario, we are psychologically primed to think of the most obvious and logical answer (e.g., what can I do next after practicing law = teach, work for the government, or go in-house). If, however, we focus on the former scenario, we can exponentially increase our optionality (e.g., how can I become an entrepreneur, how can I become a designer, or how can I become a CEO?). Thus, focusing forward can actually make us more creative.

When establishing the target position, it's important to conduct the appropriate level of diligence to create an achievable goal. Yes, there's something to be said about how startups set unrealistic goals and deadlines. But a tech startup focused on launching the latest and greatest in computing hardware is not the same as improving client service at a law firm. The timeline and percent increase must be attainable or else relationships, internally and externally, will be strained. Setting unattainable goals can also be demoralizing and kill confidence. If you are at a smaller firm, setting a goal of increasing profits by 20% can be a reasonable objective over the course of a year. This could equate to landing one major client or two medium-sized ones. If you are in biglaw, however, a 20% increase in one year can be quite unrealistic barring any anomalous deals, cases, or market conditions.

Continuing with our profit/revenue example from above, let's imagine that both Partners A and B, respectively, clarify that the problem/opportunity to be addressed is to develop a strategy to increase *revenue* by 10% over the next two years. Let's also imagine that both firms are of equal size and skill within their respective industries. Firm A focuses on tech clients where Firm B focuses on government clients. Rather than focusing on their current, respective positions, both firms focus on where they want to be in the next two years. To achieve the 10% target, Firm A decides to invest in building out a new practice area to help companies go public. Because much of Firm A's book of business consists of public tech companies, Firm A has the opportunity to leverage its experience to help smaller, private tech companies transition into the public realm (and manage all of the various public filings on an on-going basis). Firm B, on the other hand, decides to invest in strengthening its existing practices with a few heavy-weight lateral hires from the government (e.g., senators, U.S. attorneys, and senior agency personnel). As a prospect looking for representation, selecting the firm with public figures can make a big difference in your decision-making calculus. While both firms choose to embark on different pathways, both firms will work tirelessly to achieve the 10% revenue goal. If either strategy fails, the firms will course correct and develop a new strategy to hit their target. Or, if a global health pandemic necessitates working from home, both firms will leverage its virtual capabilities to charge forward with their respective plans – albeit with a few amendments.

Similar to the process of defining the problem/opportunity above, you may wish to rely on some of the creative problem-solving strategies discussed in Part II to help you identify a clear and attainable end goal (e.g., question the status quo (Section 3), identify pressure points (Section 4), embrace interdisciplinary thinking (Section 7), or learn from all parts of your business (Section 8)).

§14.4: Synchronization.

When you undergo the process of creative problem solving, you are working towards improving yourself, your team, or your organization. Successfully integrating these changes can take time and it's important to be mindful that people default to their habits. If you create a new procedure to track cases or deals, give your team enough time to form a new habit around the procedure. Contrary to popular belief, it takes more than 21 days to form a new habit. Studies show that it actually takes 66 days.[66] That's more than two months! Or, if you worked on creating a new initiative like the formation of a new shadow board, it'll take time (e.g., years) for that platform to grow into its full potential. To the extent that you can, be sure to give these new ideas and new initiatives the proper amount of time to settle in with yourself, your team, and your organization.

Relatedly, establishing key performance indicators to benchmark your progress will help provide clarity and honesty to your process. This can also help you course correct in case your implementation isn't going as planned.

In our revenue scenario from above, Firm A chose to build out a new practice area focused on taking companies public while Firm B chose to strengthen its existing practices with senior, government hires. Synchronizing the strategy within Firm A will require, among other things, ensuring: (i) that the new team works symbiotically with the existing practice groups, (ii) that marketing initiatives are effective, and (iii) that the internal teams are cross-promoting services (i.e., cross selling). To monitor the new group's progress, Partner A establishes a new integration meeting at the end of every month that brings together practice group leads to discuss progress across pre-defined key performance indicators. She also invites different groups of junior and mid-level attorneys to attend these meetings to share their experiences and provide feedback. By keeping a close eye on progress, Partner A can increase the probability that this new practice group will succeed (and hit the 10% revenue target).

For Firm B, the synchronization process looks slightly different. The focus will be on ensuring that the lateral hires are integrating well into the existing team and getting in front of clients and prospects. This will require an emphasis on socializing the laterals with the existing team so that existing members will feel comfortable picking up the phone and calling them. If one of the new hires is a former senator or the former attorney general, it can be quite intimidating to call him or her for help on a pitch if you haven't had a chance to break the ice. Additionally, rather than scheduling new monthly meetings, Partner B's existing team meetings would work effectively (as new members are being brought onto an existing team rather than bringing on an entirely new practice group like with Firm A). These regular team meetings can help Partner B keep an eye on benchmarks and progress, which will help increase Firm B's odds of success in attaining the 10% revenue target.

§15
Creativity In Law

Nothing ventured, nothing gained.

Creativity functions like an asset that yields compound interest over time – it can leave you with exponential growth if you decide to make the investment. You can learn to see your practice from multiple dimensions, explore options that no one has considered, create platforms and processes to scale your time, leverage efficiencies for your team and clients, and, simply, become a better practitioner.

The key points to remember from this playbook are as follows:

- **Legal practice as a business.** Law firms are businesses and legal teams are business units. Thinking about your practice from the business perspective can help you develop competitive advantages for you and your team.
- **Creativity as a value generator.** Businesses that are more creative outperform their peers financially and strategically. Adapting creative thinking to legal practice can yield the same benefits.
- **Action is the central tenet to creativity.** Getting your hands dirty is fundamental to creative thinking and creative problem solving. Get out there and test out new ideas.
- **Creative process.** Creativity is a collaborative endeavor to create something new and improved. Take the status quo as the springboard for forward progress, build a team around a problem or opportunity, take the road less travelled, gain feedback from everyone, and open your mind to the unknown. Remember, added value lies where no one has travelled.
- **Success.** The foundation of success is built on the knowledge

of our failures. Don't let over-perfection hinder your progress towards a better result. Don't let over-thinking dwarf your success.

- **Fun.** Unlike working through diligence materials, creative thinking and problem solving can be fun and empowering. You'll get to work with your colleagues in a different manner and shift your focus on something fresh.

As you progress on your creative journey, celebrate your wins – regardless of how big or small. If you stumble through a rough patch, take a day to recollect and recalibrate. Success and failure are as temporary or as persistent as you allow them to be. You may not be in control of everything that happens to you, but you are in control of your responses. Respond like a champion, and you will be a champion.

Celebrate your uniqueness and embrace your differences. No one ever made an impact or was ever remembered for being the same; it's the differences that define us. Allow your creative mind to distinguish you and your team. Allow your creativity to flow through.

Appendix: Creative Exercises

Appendix: Creative Exercises

Get the juices flowing.

Developing your creative mind is much like developing your legal mind. It takes practice and time. Unless you are destined for the Supreme Court, no one walks into class on the first day of law school and intuits cold call responses. To develop the legal mindset, it takes a three-year investment plus years of legal practice to get into the right frame of mind. Similarly, to develop a creative mindset, it takes practice and time to get the right perspectives.

Google conducted a two-year study in search of the defining factors between innovative and non-innovative teams. The only distinction it found across 280 teams was psychological safety, which is a quality that exists when people feel safe opening up, feel comfortable admitting mistakes, and feel empowered to test out new ideas.[67] Psychological danger, on the other hand, is a quality that exists when people are afraid of making mistakes, discouraged from sharing their ideas, and shift blame. If the latter sounds familiar, it's because psychological danger is all too common in legal practice. To change this, establishing trust and empathy between team members is key. Thus, practicing your creativity in an environment of psychological safety can help strengthen your creativity mindset and creative confidence.

A fun way to practice your creativity is to run through a series of creativity exercises in a safe space. To do this, gather a group of your friends and peers (they don't have to be lawyers – it's actually better to have various professions represented). This can be as informal as texting or calling a friend with one of the below questions and seeing where that conversation takes you. Or, it could be as formal as calling a team meeting to discuss and brainstorm. My preferred approach? Let the ideas flow over a few drinks.

Once you have your group together, run through the below creativity prompts. As you'll note, none of them focus on legal practice qua legal practice. Inspiration comes from outside the box, and that's exactly where we will begin.

1. Re-invent the pencil. How can you re-design the ubiquitous tool to better serve a particular audience?

2. Translate the restaurant dining experience into your own home. How would you redesign "take out" to better recreate the dining experience within your home?

3. Future-proof your kitchen. How would you re-design your kitchen to work for you with a tech upgrade?

4. What best-practice can we adopt from another country in the areas of transportation, food, and hygiene?

5. How would you redefine a particular sport? Rugby, football, and soccer have numerous parallels just as tennis, squash, and racquetball do. What's another sport that can be created?

6. Create a new fusion dish. This can be discussion based or, if you are culinarily capable, try making the dish with your friends.

7. Choose a household item and modernize it. We've seen doorbells, exercise bikes, watches, and scooters updated with the latest and greatest tech over the past few years. What would you do?

8. Imagine what your day-to-day life would be like in 1,000 years.

9. Improv game. Have a conversation with your friends where the first letter of the first word of your response must progress along with the alphabet. "Adam, how are you today?" "Been better, how about you? "Couldn't agree more...." After your first iteration, rerun this game but give the conversation a theme.

10. Pitch game. Pretend that your friends are investors and you are pitching a business to them. Start with something simple like a social media company or a daycare and progress to wilder examples like a company focused on interplanetary travel or space hotels.

Now, come up with three more responses to the ones that you previously gave. It may be challenging at first, but this will help you stretch your imagination and you may surprise yourself. It's okay if your ideas are a little wacky – great ideas always seem a bit strange at first (remember when people thought it'd be crazy to order clothes online or hire strangers to drive them to their destinations?).

The above prompts are meant to get the juices flowing and they can also jumpstart some fascinating discussions. You can even raise some of these questions casually over dinner or drinks with friends. Again, practicing creative thinking isn't akin to spending long hours in the library. It's about collaboration and stretching your thinking beyond your status quo. Have fun with the process.

To translate these discussions over to your practice, you can start to ask industry specific questions. How will legal practice look in the next ten years? What about the next twenty? One hundred? What does the future of your team look like? What is no one in your field doing that they should be? If you were your competitor, how would you outplay your team? Expand your discussion group, test your ideas out on a smaller scale, pilot new programs, and begin to make an impact on your team and organization.

INDEX

Index

ENDNOTES

Endnotes

[1] "Deformation Professionnelle and the Dunning-Kruger Effect – When Expertise Isn't So Great," *Interaction Design Foundation* (November 17, 2015), https://www.interaction-design.org/literature/article/deformation-professionnelle-and-the-dunning-kruger-effect-when-expertise-isn-t-so-great.

[2] I got the idea of the economic "moat" from Warren Buffett. Tae Kim, "Warren Buffett Believes this is 'The Most Important Thing' to Find in a Business," *CNBC* (May 7, 2018), https://www.cnbc.com/2018/05/07/warren-buffett-believes-this-is-the-most-important-thing-to-find-in-a-business.html (citing Warren Buffett from a Berkshire Hathaway annual shareholders meeting in 1995 from CNBC's Warren Buffett Archive).

[3] Marc Brodherson, Jason Heller, Jesko Perrey, and David Remley, "Creativity's Bottom Line: How Winning Companies Turn Creativity into Business Value and Growth," *McKinsey Digital* (June 16, 2017), https://www.mckinsey.com/business-functions/mckinsey-digital/our-insights/creativitys-bottom-line-how-winning-companies-turn-creativity-into-business-value-and-growth.

[4] See, e.g., Deanna (Lazzaroni) Pate, "The Top Skills Companies Need Most in 2020 – And How to Learn Them," *LinkedIn Learning Blog* (January 2020), https://www.linkedin.com/business/learning/blog/top-skills-and-courses/the-skills-companies-need-most-in-2020and-how-to-learn-them (ranking "creativity" as the most in-demand skill (same as 2019)); Jennifer Liu, "The 10 Most In-Demand Soft Skills to Master if You Want a Raise, Promotion or New Job in 2020," *CNBC* (November 2019), https://www.cnbc.com/2019/11/21/10-top-soft-skills-to-master-for-2020-if-you-want-a-raise-promotion-or-new-job.html.

[5] "Creativity: The Science Behind the Madness," *Big Think* (July 2020), https://www.youtube.com/watch?v=zNHDTvqbUm4&ab_channel=BigThink (highlighting a number of neuroscientists, artists, and creatives, including Beau Lotto and Ethan Hawke).

6 "Safe Enough to Try: An Interview with Zappos CEO Tony Hsieh," *McKinsey Quarterly* (October 2017), https://www.mckinsey.com/~/media/McKinsey/Business%20Functions/Organizati on/Our%20Insights/Safe%20enough%20to%20try%20An%20interview%20with %20Zappos%20CEO%20Tony%20Hsieh/Safe-enough-to-try-An-interview-with-Zappos-CEO-Tony-Hsieh.pdf?shouldIndex=false.

7 "Interview with Tony Fadell – On Setting Constraints, Ignoring Experts & Embracing Self-Doubt," *99U* (October 2012), https://www.youtube.com/watch?v=qUVUyaEk4ks.

8 "Design Thinking," *IDEO U* (2020), https://www.ideou.com/pages/design-thinking.

9 Catherine Fredman, "The IDEO Difference," *Hemispheres Magazine - United Airlines* (2002), https://new-ideo-com.s3.amazonaws.com/assets/files/pdfs/news/hemispheres_1.pdf.

10 Ben Horowitz, *The Hard Thing About Hard Things* 120 (New York: HarperCollins 2014).

11 Tweet from Richard Branson, *Twitter* (March 27, 2014), https://twitter.com/richardbranson/status/449220072176107520.

12 Personal conversation with Mahnu Davar on January 8, 2021.

13 The principle of illusory superiority is also sometimes referred to as the superiority bias or the Dunning-Kruger effect. See, e.g., Kate Fehlhaber, "The Consequences of Illusory Superiority," *Knowing Neurons* (February 6, 2017), https://knowingneurons.com/2017/02/06/illusory-superiority/.

14 Mitchell Grant, "Strength, Weakness, Opportunity, and Threat Analysis," *Investopedia* (February 24, 2020), https://www.investopedia.com/terms/s/swot.asp.

15 The principle of illusory superiority is also sometimes referred to as the superiority bias or the Dunning-Kruger effect. See, e.g., Kate Fehlhaber, "The Consequences of Illusory Superiority," *Knowing Neurons* (February 6, 2017), https://knowingneurons.com/2017/02/06/illusory-superiority/.

16 Adam Grant, *Originals* 245 (New York: Penguin Random House 2016).

17 "David M. Rubenstein," *Carlyle* (2021), https://www.carlyle.com/about-carlyle/team/david-m-rubenstein; "On Innovation, Entrepreneurialism, and Law: A Conversation with Peter Thiel and Mark A. Lemley," *Stanford Lawyer* (May 31,

2011), https://law.stanford.edu/stanford-lawyer/articles/q-a-legal-matters-with-peter-thiel-92-ba-89-bs-89-and-mark-a-lemley-ba-88/; Jeannette L. Nolen, "Lloyd Blankfein," *Britannica* (2021), https://www.britannica.com/biography/Lloyd-Blankfein; Stacy Conradt, "30 Famous People With Law Degrees," *Mental Floss* (May 24, 2012), https://www.mentalfloss.com/article/30760/30-famous-people-law-degrees.

[18] See, e.g., Vijay Eswaran, "The Business Case for Diversity in the Workplace is Now Overwhelming," *World Economic Forum* (April 29, 2019), https://www.weforum.org/agenda/2019/04/business-case-for-diversity-in-the-workplace/.

[19] Rocio Lorenzo, Nicole Voigt, Miki Tsusaka, Matt Krentz, "How Diverse Leadership Teams Boost Innovation," *Boston Consulting Group* (January 23, 2018), https://www.bcg.com/en-us/publications/2018/how-diverse-leadership-teams-boost-innovation.

[20] Cal. Corp. Code § 301.3 and § 2115.5; "Women on Boards," *California Secretary of State* (2020), https://www.sos.ca.gov/business-programs/women-boards; Richard Blake and Courtney Mathes, "Female Directors in California-Headquartered Public Companies," *Harvard Law School Forum on Corporate Governance* (January 27, 2020), https://corpgov.law.harvard.edu/2020/01/27/female-directors-in-california-headquartered-public-companies/.

[21] "2021 Proxy Paper Guidelines: An Overview of the Glass Lewis Approach To Proxy Advice – United States," *Glass Lewis* 26 (January 13, 2021), https://www.glasslewis.com/wp-content/uploads/2020/11/US-Voting-Guidelines-GL.pdf?hsCtaTracking=7c712e31-24fb-4a3a-b396-9e8568fa0685%7C86255695-f1f4-47cb-8dc0-e919a9a5cf5b; "Proxy Voting Guidelines – United States," *ISS* 11 (November 2020) https://www.issgovernance.com/file/policy/latest/americas/US-Voting-Guidelines.pdf (effective for meetings on or after February 1, 2021).

[22] "Perkins Coie Recognized by Intel and Microsoft as Most Diverse Outside Legal Team in the US," *Legal Insider* (October 1, 2020), https://legaltechnology.com/perkins-coie-recognized-by-intel-and-microsoft-as-most-diverse-outside-legal-team-in-the-us/.

[23] Research conducted through Johns Hopkins University has shown that learning and understanding are accelerated when we work through variations of a particular task. Pablo A. Celnik, Nicholas F. Wymbs, and Amy J. Bastian, "Want to Learn a New Skill Faster? Change Up Your Practice Sessions," *Johns Hopkins Medicine News and Publications* (January 28, 2016), https://www.hopkinsmedicine.org/news/media/releases/want_to_learn_a_new_skill_faster_change_up_your_practice_sessions.

[24] Robert Root-Bernstein, Lindsay Allen, Leighanna Beach, et. al., "Arts Foster

Scientific Success: Avocations of Nobel, National Academy, Royal Society, and Sigma Xi Members," 1 *Journal of Psychology of Science and Technology* 51-63 (2008).

[25] Adam Grant, *Originals* 47 (New York: Penguin Random House 2016) (referencing "The Arts and Economic Vitality: Leisure Time Interest in Art Predicts Entrepreneurship and Innovation at Work" by Laura Niemi and Sara Cordes, which is under review for publication).

[26] Carmine Gallo, "Where Innovative Business Leaders Look for Creative Ideas," Forbes (November 26, 2017), https://www.forbes.com/sites/carminegallo/2017/11/26/where-innovative-business-leaders-look-for-creative-ideas/?sh=692296ed2159.

[27] Marion Poetz, Nikolaus Franke, and Martin Schreier, "Sometimes The Best Ideas Come From Outside Your Industry," *Harvard Business Review* (November 21, 2014), https://hbr.org/2014/11/sometimes-the-best-ideas-come-from-outside-your-industry (citing Marion Poetz, Nikolaus Franke, and Martin Schreier, "Integrating Problem Solvers from Analogous Markets in New Product Ideation," 60 *Management Science* 1063-1081 (April 2014)), http://citeseerx.ist.psu.edu/viewdoc/download;jsessionid=FBAE31F9B686275C0E2449E8A659660E?doi=10.1.1.703.6810&rep=rep1&type=pdf.

[28] Adam Grant, *Originals* 190 (New York: Penguin Random House 2016).

[29] Ed Catmul and Amy Wallace, *Creativity, Inc.: Overcoming the Unseen Forces That Stand in the Way of True Inspiration* 160 (New York: Random House 2014).

[30] Eric Ries, *The Lean Startup* 86 (New York: Currency 2011).

[31] Kevin Baldacci, "7 Customer Service Lessons from Amazon CEO Jeff Bezos," *Salesforce 360 Blog* (June 2013), https://www.salesforce.com/blog/jeff-bezos-lessons-blog/.

[32] Mark Millian, "Steve Jobs Fielded Some Customer Service Requests," *CNN Business* (November 22, 2011), https://www.cnn.com/2011/11/22/tech/innovation/jobs-excerpt-customer-service/index.html.

[33] Eric Ries, *The Lean Startup* 93 (New York: Currency 2011).

[34] "Interview with Chris Sacca of Lowercase Capital Pt. 2," *This Week in Startups* (October 9, 2012), https://www.youtube.com/watch?v=SK4ezQrTqFw.

[35] Ray Dalio, "How to Build a Company Where the Best Ideas Win," *TED* (September 6, 2017), https://www.youtube.com/watch?v=HXbsVbFAczg.

[36] Ray Dalio, *Principles: Life & Work* 312 (New York: Simon & Schuster 2017).

[37] "Design Thinking Defined," *IDEO* (2021), https://designthinking.ideo.com/.

[38] "What Is Design Thinking," IDEO (2021), https://www.ideou.com/blogs/inspiration/what-is-design-thinking.

[39] See, e.g., "What Is Design Thinking," *Wharton Knowledge* (October 2019), https://kwhs.wharton.upenn.edu/2019/10/what-is-design-thinking/ (noting how companies like PepsiCo, Airbnb, Capital One, and Nike have implemented design thinking).

[40] "Products: A Selection of Case Studies," *IDEO* (2021), https://www.ideo.com/work/products.

[41] "Products: A Selection of Case Studies," *IDEO* (2021), https://www.ideo.com/work/products.

[42] See, e.g., "Nordstrom Innovation Lab: Rethinking How You Shop," *Harvard Business School* (November 22, 2015), https://digital.hbs.edu/platform-digit/submission/nordstrom-innovation-lab-rethinking-how-you-shop/; "Why We All Need More Design Thinking," *Forbes* (January 14, 2010), https://www.forbes.com/2010/01/14/tim-brown-ideo-leadership-managing-design.html?sh=1c6448621f8f (discussing Bank of America); "Understanding Human Centered Design," *Venture Forward* (May 29, 2019), https://www.ventureforwardnow.org/reimagine/2019/5/29/understanding-human-centered-design-6-part-series; and "From Design Thinking to Creative Confidence," *IDEO U* (2021), https://www.ideou.com/blogs/inspiration/from-design-thinking-to-creative-confidence.

[43] Talk by Tom Kelley, "Field Observations with Fresh Eyes," *Stanford eCorner* (July 8, 2011), https://www.youtube.com/watch?v=XrpAveg7ZIg.

[44] "The Legal Design Lab," Stanford Law School (2021), https://law.stanford.edu/organizations/pages/legal-design-lab/.

[45] "Innovation in Practice," *University of Pennsylvania School of Law* (2021), https://goat.law.upenn.edu/cf/coursefinder/course-details/?course=innovation-in-practice&sec=LAW%20541001&term=2020C&page=1.

[46] "Porter's 5 Forces," Investopedia (February 22, 2020), https://www.investopedia.com/terms/p/porter.asp.

[47] "Diffusion of Innovation Theory," *Boston University* (September 9, 2019), https://sphweb.bumc.bu.edu/otlt/mph-modules/sb/behavioralchangetheories/behavioralchangetheories4.html.

[48] Eric Ries, *The Lean Startup* 93 (New York: Currency 2011).

[49] Jim Collins, *Good to Great* (New York: HarperCollins 2001).

[50] "Interview with Jack Dorsey, Twitter Co-Founder Jack Dorsey's Advice to Innovators," *CBS This Morning* (March 6, 2012), https://www.youtube.com/watch?v=V76ey3Ug8pM.

[51] Eric Ries, *Lean Startup* 56 (New York: Currency 2011).

[52] "Interview with Mark Zuckerberg, Startup School 2013," *Y Combinator* (October 25, 2013), https://www.youtube.com/watch?v=MGsalg2f9js.

[53] Ray Dalio, *Principles: Life & Work* 348 (New York: Simon & Schuster 2017).

[54] Ray Dalio, *Principles: Life & Work* 351 (New York: Simon & Schuster 2017).

[55] "Interview with Sara Blakely – Spanx Founder: My Dad Encouraged Me to Fail," *CNN Business* (March 30, 2018), https://www.youtube.com/watch?v=_TeV9op6Mp8.

[56] Sylvester Stallone as Rocky Balboa, *Rocky Balboa* (Metro-Goldwyn-Mayer, Columbia Pictures, Revolution Studios, Chartoff/Winkler Productions 2006).

[57] "Teaching Tip Sheet: Self-Efficacy," *American Psychological Association* (2009), https://www.apa.org/pi/aids/resources/education/self-efficacy.

[58] Angela Duckworth, "Cultivating Confidence: Succeeding One Step at a Time," *Character Lab* (December 6, 2020), https://characterlab.org/tips-of-the-week/cultivating-confidence/.

[59] Ben Horowitz, *The Hard Thing About Hard Things* 88 (New York: HarperCollins 2014).

[60] Yoda, *Star Wars Episode V: The Empire Strikes Back* (Lucasfilm Ltd. 1980).

[61] "Interview with Elon Musk, The First Principles Method Explained," *Innomind* (December 4, 2013), https://www.youtube.com/watch?v=NV3sBlRgzTI&ab_channel=innomind.

[62] René Descartes, *Discourse on the Method of Rightly Conducting Ones Reason and of Seeking Truth in the Sciences* IV (1637).

[63] Daniel Marlin, "How the World's Smartest People Learn Things Faster," *Entrepreneur* (April 21, 2017), https://www.entrepreneur.com/article/292986.

[64] Sarah Zielinski, "The Secrets of Sherlock's Mind Palace," *Smithsonian Magazine* (February 3, 2014), https://www.smithsonianmag.com/arts-

culture/secrets-sherlocks-mind-palace-180949567/. The "mind palace" is also known as the method of loci, the memory theater, and the memory palace.

65 Richard C. Mohs, "How to Improve Your Memory: The Method of Loci," *How Stuff Works* (2021), https://health.howstuffworks.com/human-body/systems/nervous-system/how-to-improve-your-memory7.htm.

66 Gretchen Rubin, "Stop Expecting to Change Your Habit in 21 Days," *Psychology Today* (October 21, 2009), https://www.psychologytoday.com/us/blog/the-happiness-project/200910/stop-expecting-change-your-habit-in-21-days.

67 "This is the Way Google & IDEO Foster Creativity," *IDEO U* (September 29, 2017), https://www.ideou.com/blogs/inspiration/how-google-fosters-creativity-innovation.

www.ingramcontent.com/pod-product-compliance
Lightning Source LLC
Chambersburg PA
CBHW060619200326
41521CB00007B/817